NOT EVERYTHING IN (

'Such a good book! It clears away the undergrowth of tradition to reveal hidden treasure, so that the Bible reads like new. Best of all, fresh understandings emerge that have to do directly with the mission of the church today.'

Dr Jonathan Ingleby
Head of Mission Studies, Redcliffe College

'Provocative? Yes, but refreshing and entirely biblical! A book to blow away the cobwebs in places where our windows have been closed and there is no through draught. Neil Rees's unashamed objective is to remove any hindrance or barrier which may exist in our minds towards the fulfilment of the Great Commission. I heartily recommend his book as a challenge to think differently and to think biblically about mission and the support of those involved.'

John Noble
Church planter and leader

'Don't be fooled by the title of this book. It has not been written with the intent of undermining the inspiration or authority of the Scriptures. Quite the reverse. Neil wants to see the Scriptures released from trappings that can so easily prevent the message of God being clearly understood by those who need to hear it.'

Philip Vogel
Church planter and leader

'Fasten your seat belts for a turbulent ride that will challenge your presuppositions and cause you to review how you study God's Word. Neil Rees speaks directly into our comfort zones, as his sharp missional perspective shapes our thinking to a more biblical standard. He carefully explains the way things were written and encourages us as to how we can apply ageless truth in our current culture.'

Dave Richards
Salt and Light Ministries

'I enjoyed this book and thoroughly recommend it. Do not be put off by the title. It has a disarming freshness and originality and I believe will open up your understanding of the Bible. I was left even more convinced of the inspiration of the Bible.'

Norman Warren
author of Journey Into Life

'This is a very important book. There is no more important book to know all about than the Bible, and this book will tell you many, many things which 98% of Christ's followers don't know and have never even thought about.'

Ralph D. Winter
Chancellor, William Carey International University

Not Everything in Our Bibles Is Inspired

NEIL REES

KINGSWAY PUBLICATIONS
EASTBOURNE

For my parents, David and Joan,
in recognition of their love and total commitment to me
since the day I was born.

Contents

Acknowledgements

Being a product of this digital age, there is no one to thank for the typing! But my sincere thanks do go to the following:

Dr Ralph Winter and the staff at William Carey International University, whose World Christian Foundations programme provided much of the insight and stimulus to ongoing thought that has gone into my writing.

David Botelho and the team of Missão Horizontes, Brazil, for the initial challenge to write this book.

Bridget Shelmerdine for her work in translating from the original Spanish.

Staff at Kingsway for their help in preparing for publication this edition for English-speaking readers.

My companions in church and mission in Spain who have suffered with me as we have grown in Jesus, and who, without realising it, have been the testing ground for much of what is contained in this book.

Those who, throughout my life with the Lord, have contributed, in person or through their writings, to my discipleship and growth as a believer. If I have learned anything, I owe it to them.

My wife and my two children, who share with me the reality of living to be a blessing to the nations.

The Lord, who brought me into his way, and granted me the privilege of being his co-worker amongst the peoples of the world.

Foreword

What you have in your hands is a jewel. On the one hand it is a light, jaunty page-turner, almost like reading a novel. At the same time it is constantly wandering (cleverly, intentionally) into a huge amount of the kind of information about the Bible that is normally reserved for privileged seminary students.

I truly doubt if anyone has ever written a book which makes so much 'weighty' knowledge about the Bible so digestible, so accessible, so fascinating and so attractive. It is not to be read just once, but treasured as a permanent reference to which you will want to refer again and again.

I suspect if Neil had given chapter titles that employed seminary language to describe their contents, you, the reader, might be inclined to skip this one or that one. As it is, you can't possibly imagine what is in a chapter simply by reading its title! But that is a very good thing. No serious believer ought to skip even a single chapter. Once you get into a chapter you find yourself involved in information you might never have sought out – mainly because you could not have imagined what it was.

This is a very important book. It is very important for the simple reason that the Bible itself is very important. There is no more important book to know all about than the Bible, and this book will tell you many, many things which 98 per cent of Christ's followers don't know and have never even thought about.

Good work, Neil. You have created an incredibly valuable introduction to the Bible, and you have done it in a marvellously winsome way. It is bound to be a major blessing to many.

Ralph D. Winter
Chancellor, William Carey International University

1

Not Everything in Our Bibles Is Inspired by God

Not everything in our Bibles is inspired by God. And take note, I am an orthodox evangelical, or at least I think I am. I believe in 1 Timothy 3:16, and in the infallibility of the Scriptures. I accept the Bible as the Word of God. But I still maintain that not everything in *our* Bibles is inspired by God.

Like the concordance, for example. Or the glossary. Or the maps, the introduction, the tables of weights and measures, the footnotes, the cross references and studies, the abbreviations, the ISBN number or the copyright notice on the title page, the page on 'how to find help when. . .', or the golden letters embossed onto the leather cover, along with a number of other things we will look at in the course of this book. And, if we are honest, even the translation itself isn't inspired – being the expression in English of divine thought revealed in the writings of inspired biblical authors, each one writing in his native language; that is, Hebrew, Aramaic, or Greek.

Thankfully, today we have a wide variety of Bibles, translations for all possible tastes, study editions, with commentaries and concordances, along with assorted notes – the accumulated wisdom of today's most widely recognised scholars all made available to us. And, as if this were not enough, information technology now provides us with new methods of studying the meaning of words in the original languages, comparing translations, and a thousand and one other ways of getting even more out of the Bible, the Word of God.

But in this avalanche of information, which the majority of the time without doubt helps us to get closer to the original meaning of the eternally relevant Word of God, we must not forget the fact that some of these 'helps' can hide small but important details of God's original revelation in the Bible. The purpose of this book is to help readers to remove one or other of these impositions on the Word of God, and to look at generally very well-known texts in a new light, discovering hitherto unnoticed meanings.

It is my hope and my prayer that in this way we will be able to come just that bit closer to the author of this Word of life, the Lord Jesus Christ, and know a little more of his heart for a world that has not yet come to know him. His desire to draw together his bride from all across this world is revealed to us on every page of the Bible. I shall consider my purpose fulfilled if, when reaching the end of this short work, readers have understood something more of the missionary heart of God and can offer their own heart, even their whole life, in service to our Lord. To him be glory, now and for ever.

And finally, please do be assured that the title is only

meant to shock a little, and that I believe in the inspiration of Scripture as much as you do. Don't worry – you are not holding a further attempt to 'reveal the Bible's faults'. As the Scriptures themselves say, not one jot or tittle – in other words, not an accent or a pen stroke – will be removed from them, until all that is written in them is fulfilled.

Oh, and just in case you hadn't noticed, this chapter is actually the introduction to the rest of the book. But, as you probably well know, very few people read the 'introduction', and even fewer read a 'preface', so I decided to disguise the introduction as the first chapter. I hope you will be able to forgive these underhand tactics, and that you will be able to enjoy the rest of the book fully aware of its purpose and the context in which it has been written.

2

'Chapter One'

It was the first time I had set foot in an evangelical church since leaving my mother's Methodist church at the ripe old age of 12. The fact that I was prepared to darken the doorstep of such an unknown place says something about my desire to continue pursuing a possible date, but nothing about my desire to pursue the 'things of God'. I thus found myself in a Bible study on death. Not a bad subject for a beginner. Someone placed a rather large volume in my hands, and the passage that was to serve as the starting place for our study was announced: 'First Corinthians, chapter 15.'

I had not yet learned the art that Christians seem to have developed to perfection of not using the contents page or index when they don't know where to find a book of the Bible, so I found the book in question quite quickly. And while we are on the subject, this is something I have never really understood. Why are we so opposed to using the index of our Bibles? Maybe it's because we think that others will realise we don't read our Bibles enough. But come on, finding Nahum is never easy, even for the most 'Biblewormy' believers. Instead, however, we open our

Bibles and quickly flick through the pages, as if that particular book isn't in the same place we left it last time. At the same time, we give ourselves a crick in the neck with those casual sideways glances at the person sitting next to us, to try and get a rough idea of where the book is, but without anyone seeing us. How naïve we are – this 'controlled dither' over the pages of our Bibles gives us away much more than the use of the index.

But let's get to the point. What was this 'chapter' they were referring to? I was used to chapters in normal books, with a title at the top, on a new page, and generally with a space at the end of the previous chapter. According to my experience to date, the very 'books' of the Bible seemed more like conventional 'chapters'. Nevertheless, I then noticed the numbers in large print spread at intervals through the text, and I learned how to do it properly. I had discovered how to follow chapters in the Bible, and it didn't take me long to get the hang of verses too. (What a 'smart Alec'!)

Chapters. As you will have noticed, the Bible is divided into chapters. But it wasn't always like that: they were added long after each book had been written. As I have said, not everything in our Bibles is inspired by God. Let's start by looking at these chapter divisions.

We do not possess any 'original' manuscripts of the Bible. Not that we know of, at any rate. The originals, known as 'autographs', those texts written by the biblical authors on rolls of parchment or papyrus, disappeared many years ago. What we have today is a text based on the thousands and thousands of copies which were made of these original texts over the course of the centuries.

By saying this I do not want to insinuate that our biblical

text is not trustworthy. Far from it. The reliability of our current text has been amply demonstrated, but it would go beyond the bounds of this study to enter into any more details. Thanks to God, today we possess texts that are fully trustworthy, preserved throughout history according to the will of God, and we can be confident that the text used as the basis for modern Bible translations is essentially the same text as that which was inspired and written down so many years ago. Where there are doubts, they are minimal and do not affect the meaning of the Scriptures in any way, nor the fundamental body of Christian doctrine.

Nevertheless, neither the original texts – the 'autographs' inspired by God – nor the first copies of these which circulated in the early church looked the same as our modern Bibles. Let's look more closely at the Greek writings which make up the New Testament. Initially, the text was written on rolls of papyrus solely in capitals, with no accents, or punctuation marks, or even spaces between the words. It goes without saying, then, that the current division into chapters and verses was totally absent. Texts were normally written solely in capital letters, in columns with the same number of letters in each, distributed along the length of a roll of parchment or papyrus. It would be something like the following paragraph:

```
READINGABIBLICALWRITINGATT      RENOFULLSTOPSNORCOMMASN
HATTIMEWASNOTSUCHANEASYT        OREVENCAPITALLETTERSTOMA
ASKITWASNECESSARYTOKNOWT        RKTHEBEGINNINGOFASENTENCE
HELANGUAGEWELLITSVOCABUL        MADEREADINGITQUITEALOTMO
ARYITSGRAMMARINORDERTOBE        RECOMPLICATEDITHINKTHATEN
ABLETOUNDERSTANDWHATATE         OUGHHASBEENSAIDTOENABLEE
XTSAIDTHEFACTTHATTHEREWE        VERYONETOSEEWHATIMEAN
```

Well, I'm glad that's clear now. (For those who have honestly not been able to decipher these columns, or for those who are too lazy to try, or for life's incorrigible cheats, I have transcribed this text at the end of the chapter.)

Even though very soon parchments gathered into books called 'codices' began to be used, this practice continued on the pages of these books until about the ninth century and is reflected in the best manuscripts available today, known as 'uncials'. Copying these manuscripts was, however, a slow process, and the demand for Bibles already created a demand for new methods. As they were unable to turn to computers and laser printers, or even the most basic printing press, each copy had to be done by hand. So a cursive, joined-up handwritten script developed, a style which started to become common from about the tenth century, in those manuscripts which are today known as 'minuscules'.

Spaces between words had started to be used as early as the sixth century and, in the centuries that followed, scribes availed themselves of punctuation, accents, other aids to pronunciation, and even question marks. But none of these were part of the original, inspired text.

We will return to this matter of the lack of punctuation later. What interests us now is the division of the biblical text into chapters.

When Paul wrote a letter to a congregation, it was a letter, nothing less and nothing more. I doubt that Paul ever imagined that a couple of thousand years later, millions of people all around the world would be reading what he had written from prison in Rome to the congregation at Philippi, for example. He would have had a hard job grasping the fact that thousands of pages of studies would be written about his works, and that believers of all nations would send one another quotes from what were his personal letters to encourage one congregation. Amazing.

He wrote his letters in the same way as we write today. In other words, he sat down at his computer, switched the screen on, and. . . OK, OK. Let's try again without any modern technological tools. We get a sheet of paper, and a pen or pencil, and write: 'Dear friend. . .' And so we carry on, expressing our thoughts until we get to the end. 'God bless, lots of love, Neil.' We don't think of dividing our letter into 'chapters', much less 'verses', so that the text can be studied more easily, or so that future readers can refer to different parts without confusion. Of course not. We write, and that's that.

This is what Paul did too, along with the other biblical writers. They wrote their different works thinking of the people who were to receive them, and without attempting to give their writings any special format to make them more presentable for later. All the divisions that are found in the Bible text are subsequent additions and do not form part of the inspired text.

Well, not all of them, but generally speaking that is the reality of the biblical text. The only divisions as such which can be considered part of the 'autographs', or original texts, are the natural divisions between the psalms, which are presented as separate songs, the majority of which have their own title. This division can be seen even more clearly in those psalms which are acrostic poems, where each 'verse' starts with a consecutive letter of the Hebrew alphabet – for example, Psalms 9 and 10 together, 25, 34, 37 and 112, amongst others. Or in Psalm 119, in which all the lines in one verse (in the poetic sense of the word, rather than the biblical sense) start with the same Hebrew letter, and continue thus consecutively through the 22 verses. The whole book of Lamentations (except the last chapter) also uses this system.

Apart from these natural divisions which stem from the literary style used, there are no divisions in the original text of the Bible. Where, then, do we get the divisions that are used in our Bibles today?

The Torah or Pentateuch (the first five books of the Bible) was divided into sections called *sedarim* before the exile, and some 54 sections known as *parashiyyoth* were elaborated during the captivity in Babylon. Later on other, smaller divisions were added. In the same way, in the second century BC, divisions known as *haftaroth*, which corresponded to the *sedarim* of the Pentateuch, were added by the Maccabees in the books of the prophets.

The Masoretes, the Jewish scribes who preserved and copied the text of the Old Testament, added vowels to the Hebrew text from the tenth century onwards, and then began to put symbols in the margins of the texts to indicate the start of a new 'chapter'. These divisions became generally accepted around the year 1330. The first edition of the Old Testament in Hebrew with markers for chapters and verses was published in the year 1571.

And, departing slightly from the outline for this chapter, here is another point worth mentioning: consider the vowels in the Scriptures which were written in Hebrew and Aramaic. The inspired text of the Old Testament was written entirely without vowels, and this can add to the difficulty of understanding it. Like the majority of languages of the Semitic family, Hebrew can be understood quite well when written without vowels, but sometimes it leaves room for a little confusion. But at least it isn't like writing English with no vowels. We would never know whether 'VNDFNCMTMYDRTHMST' was meant to read, 'A vain deaf one came to my door the most,' or, 'I've no idea if Eunice met my dear Thomas too.'

That is why different translations of certain verses in the Old Testament can vary significantly, without giving us cause to complain about the team of translators. Thus Psalm 73:4 can be correctly translated, 'For there are no bands in their death: but their strength is firm' (AV). But by dividing the Hebrew slightly differently, it can be translated equally well as, 'They have no struggles, their bodies are healthy and strong' (NIV). A more extreme example can be found in Numbers 24:23. Here the prophet Balaam says, 'Ah, who can live when God does this?' But, again using a different division of the Hebrew, it could perfectly well be translated as, 'A people will gather from the north.'

The strangest of all is Proverbs 30:1. The NIV renders it, 'This man declared to Ithiel, to Ithiel and to Ucal,' but recognises that with a different word division it could read, 'This man declared, "I am weary, O God; I am weary, O God, and faint."' The GNB echoes something of this sentiment too: 'God is not with me, God is not with me, and I am helpless.' What variety. But if we carry on like this we'll never finish this chapter. Let's get back to the matter in hand, the chapters. . .

And what about the divisions of chapters and verses in the New Testament? Before the Nicene Council (AD 325) there were already sections known as *kefalaia*, but these did not correspond to the present-day chapter divisions. A completely different system – which doesn't correspond to our chapters either – was used in the Codex Vaticanus of the fourth century (referred to in theological treatises by the letter 'B'). And yet another system (which, yes, you've guessed it, also had nothing to do with our present-day chapters) was used by Eusebius of Caesarea. These sections were longer than our verses but shorter than our chapters.

These divisions were gradually modified through the centuries, and finally in the thirteenth century by a professor of the University of Paris called Stephen Langton, later Archbishop of Canterbury. (To be fair, it should be mentioned that some give the credit for this work to a certain French Cardinal, Hugo de St Cher.) And so the chapters which were used in future editions of the Bible came into being, beginning with the Wycliffe Bible of 1382, which provided the basis for subsequent translations and versions and so came to be the (almost) universal system. The verses came later on, and their history will be examined a little later on in this book. For now we'll stay with the chapters.

The fact is that it sometimes seems as if the aforementioned scholar, Stephen Langton, was mistaken in choosing the best place to divide up the biblical text. Let's look at Mark 9, for example. Shouldn't this chapter start with verse 2, just as it does in the parallel passage in Matthew 17? The same could be said of Hosea 2, 1 Samuel 7, or 1 Corinthians 11. Then there's Exodus 8, which would be better starting off with the previous verse (the last one of chapter 7), or Acts 8, which starts (in my opinion, of course) half a verse too early. I'm sure everyone could add to this illustrative list.

Very interesting, but so what? Why so much fuss about the divisions imposed upon the inspired text of the Bible? Does it really matter? Does it subtract anything from the reading of the Word of God? Well, yes, sometimes it does.

As we have seen, the authors wrote their message following one line of thought from beginning to end. This especially applies in the case of the books of the New Testament, which are generally shorter than those of the Old Testament and have a specific target. They were written to be read in one go, from the first word to the last, without stopping. They were not theological treatises to be subjected to minute analysis, nor were they 'devotional' books which can be chopped into 'daily Bible morsels'. They contain clear, direct messages written to concrete, historical people.

If you have never done it, why don't you make yourself a cup of tea or coffee, or whatever you like to drink, and sit down and read a whole book of the New Testament in one go? Try it with Mark, and you will discover a book full of action at a pace worthy of an action movie. Or take the book of 1 Corinthians, and you will see the apostle's development of his argument. Or Revelation – maybe you won't understand every word, every image, but you will be left with a sense of the greatness of our God, and his final control over events in a volatile and unstable world.

However, our habits of devotional reading and thematic preaching make us consider the Bible in chunks, and we tend to lose the bird's-eye view of the central message of every book. Doing 'biblical gymnastics', leapfrogging from page to page during a sermon, is not a bad thing now and then, but it does not allow us to grasp the essence of each book – each one an independent act of revelation – and it deprives us of something fundamental if it becomes the norm in our churches. Even expository preaching can fall down here, if time is not dedicated not only to the passage in question, but also to its connection with the previous one, the next one, and to how it contributes to developing the whole message of the book.

And what about 'devotional' reading? These days, how can we dedicate time to reading the Word of God? The Lord can manage to speak to us in 10 or 15 minutes a day, can't he? A passage to be read every day, maybe a few study questions, a few prayers, and we're done. And what should we read? Most of us probably read a chapter, or maybe even less. And if we're really making an effort we could read a couple of chapters. Or even four, if we're trying to read the whole Bible in a year. And if we use a devotional help it's very likely that it will give us one chapter, or perhaps a few verses.

What more does the Lord want from us? Perhaps a serious effort to understand 'correctly the message of God's truth' (2 Timothy 2:15, GNB), and a dedication to the study of his Word in the same basic units in which he revealed it to us – whole books. If we only ever read the Bible chapter by chapter when God revealed it differently, we will certainly lose part of what he wants to say to us.

Let's consider a serious and important example, and the one which inspired me to write this chapter. But, to help you better understand the phenomenon I am describing, we'll do it in the next chapter.

*   *   *

As promised, here is the text of the paragraph which was written in capital letters in two columns, and without spaces between the words, as early biblical manuscripts were written:

> Reading a biblical writing at that time was not such an easy task. It was necessary to know the language well – its vocabulary, its grammar – in order to be able to understand what a text said. The fact that there were no full stops, nor commas, nor even capital letters to mark the beginning of a sentence, made reading it quite a lot more complicated. I think that enough has been said to enable everyone to see what I mean.

3

'And I Looked for a Man Among Them'

What's your favourite chapter of the Bible? I'm sure more than one reader will say Romans 8. What a chapter! Tremendous stuff. Living by the Spirit . . . the security of being a son of God . . . all things work together for my good (if I truly love God, of course) . . . 'if God is for us' . . . 'who shall separate us from the love of Christ?' . . . 'we are more than conquerors'. We reach the end of this chapter with those powerful words which have brought peace and comfort to generations of believers:

> For I am convinced that neither death nor life, neither angels nor demons, neither the present nor the future, nor any powers, neither height nor depth, nor anything else in all creation, will be able to separate us from the love of God that is in Christ Jesus our Lord. (Romans 8:38–39)

Hallelujah! We draw a deep breath, close our Bibles and, lifting our faces towards heaven with a smile of pure contentment, we give thanks to God for such promises, such security. 'Thank you, Lord. You are so good.'

And of course he is. But that's not what we're looking at

now. We carry on to spend the day going about our business, go to bed and dream sweet dreams, and the next day we turn to our Bibles again and open them at Romans 9. We start to read, but we make no connection with what we read yesterday, or a few days ago if we haven't been very faithful in our reading. The joy and the security, the tremendous feeling of privilege at being a son of God, are left behind.

Now we read:

> I speak the truth in Christ – I am not lying, my conscience confirms it in the Holy Spirit – I have great sorrow and unceasing anguish in my heart. For I could wish that I myself were cursed and cut off from Christ for the sake of my brothers, those of my own race, the people of Israel. (Romans 9:1–3)

We think of Paul, his burden for his people the Israelites, his desire to bless them, and we give thanks to God for his example.

But what connection is there between this desire to be cursed by God, even separated from Christ, and the security he felt just a few verses before? And what does it have to do with us? If we don't take these words from Romans 9 in their context immediately following the dramatic conclusion to Romans 8, we lose the force of what it is saying to us.

Paul has no doubt about the goodness and faithfulness of God, nor about his own security as a believer in Christ. What can separate us from his love? Nothing! We are secure in him, completely secure. Nothing can get in the way of our relationship with him. Nothing created, nothing in the human nor the spiritual world, not even the devil, nothing in the future, whatever it contains, nor even death itself.

We are secure, 100 per cent secure in his love and his commitment to us. He loves us, he loved us, he gave his Son to save us, and he has no intention of letting anything separate us from him now. Praise the Lord!

However, it doesn't end there. Paul did not finish writing 'chapter 8' like this, then have a rest and go back to writing the ninth chapter as if it were totally disconnected from what had gone before. No – he continued with his line of thought, and he teaches us a profound lesson on the purpose of God for his children.

The security which we have as believers in the love of our heavenly Father should lead us to surrender ourselves to him and his purposes for a world which still has not experienced the privilege of knowing him. To understand – and more, to experience – this security makes us conscious of the tremendous abyss which separates those who do not know God from all that is available to us in his forgiveness. It should give birth to a burning desire in the heart of the believer to do everything in our power to help our friends and family enter and enjoy the blessings of a relationship with God.

Paul goes even further. The one who is love causes that love with which he has loved us to well up in the hearts of his children – that same love which inspired him to give his own Son over to death, from whom he had never been and could never be separated. That love which motivated Jesus, contemplating a lost humanity with no possibility of returning to his arms, to say to the Father, 'Yes, Father, I will go.' That love which leads the eternal Spirit to establish his dwelling place within hard and rebellious hearts like ours. A love which offers itself unto death, in order to be able to win the object in its view. Love which does not waver before the high cost, the personal sacrifice, the tremendous implications of its actions. It loves, continues to love, and will always love.

Paul's longing for his people reaches the level of God's own love for us. He wishes to lose what cannot be lost, if in doing so his people could find the salvation which he has experienced. He does not offer up an 'easy' prayer. He indicates his desire to spend eternity without Christ, to be *anathema*, or 'cursed', if only it would help his people to come to know God in his Son Jesus Christ. Paul is teaching us the mystery of true intercession.

Intercession is not 'praying lots', 'spending much time praying', or 'praying even more'. It's not even 'more intensive prayer'. We can pray for many people and many situations. We pray, and that's it. We go back to our work having 'fulfilled' our duty (or desire), leaving the results of our prayers up to God. It costs us no more than the time we spend in prayer, and sometimes a broken heart for a while.

But intercession is not like that. It is another dimension of prayer, in which those who pray become inextricably linked with the objects of their prayers. Intercession unites us in a mysterious yet real way not only with God, but also with those for whom we are praying. A bond is formed between the 'pray-ers' and the 'targets' of their prayers, in which we want to become completely identified with them, and join our eternal destiny to theirs.

That's what happened to Moses all those years ago, when he received a very tempting offer from God. And what an offer. After so much suffering and so much disappointment with the Lord's people, not to mention what was still to come, Moses must have had enough of them. He must have known what he was in for. And it seemed he was not the only one who was getting a bit fed up. In anticipation of the unforgettable words of the Lord Jesus himself more than 1,000 years later, 'O unbelieving and perverse generation . . . how long shall I stay with you? How long shall I put up with you?' (Matthew 17:17), Yahweh expresses himself to Moses thus: 'I know how stubborn these people are. Now, don't try to stop me. I am angry with them, and I am going to destroy them. Then I will make you and your descendants into a great nation' (Exodus 32:9–10 GNB).

I don't know how many of our pastors and leaders today would have been able to resist such a tempting offer. You're not just released from a heavy burden, but also you achieve a certain amount of personal success. At least we would ask for time to think about it. Let's be honest, how many of us would have acted as Moses did? But just what did Moses do? First, he 'set himself to placate the LORD his God' (v. 11 REB). He starts reasoning with God. He decides to try and convince him not to do it, reminding him of his own words and promises to his people. And he persuades him to give up the idea.

So far so good. Praying the promises of God, persisting in prayer, these are things we know. But we are wrong if we imagine that Moses' commitment to prayer for the people of Israel ends there. He comes down from the mountain, from the presence of God, and walks among the people, allowing their reality to touch him to the bone. From there he returns to the presence of God – 'perhaps I can obtain forgiveness for your sin' (v. 30 GNB). And now he teaches us another lesson about true intercession. He presents himself before the presence of God again and says, 'Oh, what a great sin these people have committed! They have made themselves gods of gold. But now, please forgive their sin – but if not, then blot me out of the book you have written' (v. 32).

'Forgive them, Lord.' I think all of us are capable of praying this. 'Do not count this sin against them.' Thus far we are dealing with simple prayer. 'And if you won't forgive them, I don't want you to forgive me either.' This is where the real intercession starts. 'I want my eternity to be theirs; for you to do the same thing with me as you do with them, and with them the same as you do with me.' The intercessor identifies himself with the people, no longer crying out to God from the perspective of a spectator, but as one fully implicated in the matter.

Now, let's just make clear what we are talking about here. This is not about whether we can or can't lose our salvation, nor whether we can 'bargain' with God, as if our relationship with him were a stronger currency. Of course not. As we saw with Paul, intercession is carried out from the perspective of total security in our relationship with God. And God's answer to Moses, that he would blot out only 'whoever has sinned against me' (v. 33), is an indication of his response to intercession. It is primarily about the heart of the intercessor, the type of commitment to God which really can change history.

That's how it was with Moses. He had identified himself with the people to such an extent that he lived that commitment from that moment on, throughout his earthly pilgrimage. Months later, when at the entrance to the promised land they rebelled against God and refused to believe and enter into the land that he was giving them, the Lord got angry with them again. Again he threatens to destroy them and makes Moses an offer: 'I will make you into a nation greater and stronger than they' (Numbers 14:12). But again Moses gets before God to prevent him from doing it.

In the end, Moses even loses his own entry into the promised land because of his insistence on not abandoning the Israelites, but accompanying them to see the promises of God fulfilled in them. True intercession has its price, and Moses was prepared to pay it.

Let's not think that Moses was the only one who knew what real intercession was. Like a good discipler, he transmitted this ministry to others. In Numbers 16 we read a remarkable story which shows us the intercession of Aaron as well. As in the majority of Christian groups, there was grumbling and discontentment towards the leadership. Korah and a few others decide to throw out Moses and Aaron, accusing them of abusing their privileges as leaders. (If they had only known how Moses had responded to the offer the Lord had made him!) 'OK,' says Moses, 'let's have an election. Whoever God doesn't want as a leader, the ground will open up and swallow him. And whoever is left is the one God has chosen.' (Sometimes it's very tempting to try and apply this same 'electoral' process to the conflicts arising in our day in the church; it would undoubtedly reduce the number of complaints about our activities as leaders. . .)

And that's what happened. The ground opened and swallowed Korah, his companions, his family and all his

belongings. And that was the end of it . . . or was it? Well,
no. The next day the Israelites seem to have forgotten the
exact details surrounding the events. They start to accuse
Moses and Aaron: 'You have killed some of the LORD's
people.' (What short memories we have – of course nothing like this ever happens today. . .) God can't stand any
more, and orders Moses and Aaron: 'Stand back from these
people, and I will destroy them on the spot!' (Numbers
16:41–45 GNB).

This is serious stuff – by the end of the story nearly
15,000 would have shuffled off this mortal coil. Moses sees
what is happening and comments, 'Wrath has come out
from the LORD; the plague has started' (v. 46). There is no
time to start reasoning with God, or to call a prayer meeting
for Thursday evening at eight o'clock. They have to act,
right now. It's urgent and the situation calls for decisive
action. Enter Aaron, acting under the direction of Moses
and on his authority.

He 'ran' to where the people were – that is, into the midst
of the plague – and 'offered the incense and made atone-
ment for them' (v. 47). He begins to offer up prayer on
behalf of this rebellious people who deserve what is coming
to them. But again this is not all, and it goes much further
than just his desire to see the plague stop. With an action
worthy of the bravest of heroes, Aaron 'stood between the
living and the dead' (v. 48). What faith. What love. What
devotion.

Put yourself in his shoes for a moment. Live it. Make a
video in your mind and experience this incredible moment
with Aaron. God has already made known his will, that he
wants to destroy all the people and bless you and your

brother. All around you people are dropping like flies, and you dare to run into the centre of this battleground and put yourself in between God with his wrath and those of the people who are still alive. 'God, if you want to kill them, you'll have to kill me too. If you carry on with this plague, it will be over my dead body. Come on, kill me! And if you don't want to kill me, then you'll have to forgive these people their transgression.'

Did Aaron know before he went out there what was going to happen? Could he be certain he would return to Moses alive? I don't know, but I can see that it didn't matter to him. There's the intercessor, ready to pay a real price so that people don't receive the destruction they deserve. And 'the plague stopped. But 14,700 people died' (vv. 48, 49). Praise God for the importunity of the intercessor.

There is another, much greater than Moses and Aaron, who can teach us about intercession – the Lord Jesus Christ. It was his principal ministry during his life on earth and continues to be his principal activity in heaven: 'Who is he that condemns? Christ Jesus, who died – more than that, who was raised to life – is at the right hand of God and is also interceding for us' (Romans 8:34). As Hebrews 7:25 also teaches us, 'he always lives to intercede for them'. In this way he fulfils Job's heart's desire: 'I want someone to plead with God for me, as one pleads for a friend' (Job 16:21 GNB).

Jesus did not just pray for us – he did not just stay in heaven offering prayers to his Father. He entered our lives, he identified 100 per cent with us, took part in our reality, making it his, in order to make his reality ours.

> Therefore I will give him a portion among the great,
>   and he will divide the spoils with the strong,
> because he poured out his life unto death,
>   and was numbered with the transgressors.
> For he bore the sin of many,
>   and made intercession for the transgressors.
> (Isaiah 53:12)

This is the reality of intercession. And it doesn't stop there. As in everything, the Lord Jesus wants to reproduce his character and his ministry in those who make up his people, by the person of the Holy Spirit who dwells in the believer. The Spirit himself makes intercession for us, and through us, as we surrender to his purposes for our lives. We do not know how we ought to pray, 'but the Spirit himself intercedes for us with groans that words cannot express' (Romans 8:26).

Jesus 'borrows' our bodies to express himself to a world that still doesn't know him. He has no hands or arms but ours with which to hug people. He has no mouth but ours through which to announce his message. He has no feet but ours to take the gospel to the four corners of the earth. But he wants our heart as well. A heart surrendered to his will and ready to pay the price of true intercession. Ready to identify itself with the needs of a people and bring them almost irremediably before God, to feel what they feel, to abandon itself to God, if only he will save them as he has saved us.

I will never forget that little town, whose name I never knew, but which is for ever engraved on my heart. It wasn't anything special. On the contrary, it was a run-down village in the middle of nowhere up in the Atlas mountains on the edge of the vast Sahara desert. But it was a town with no known witness, with no believers and with no possibility of hearing the gospel. It represented the hundreds and thousands of similar towns dotted all over the countryside of North Africa, each one full of people who needed Christ. At the top of the mountain range which overlooked the town, we stopped in the shade of a miserable shrub, to rest after our long walk and to pray for this town.

The 'romance' of the missionary life had already evaporated some time ago for me. Those first impressions, that first love, the novelty, the adorable children, the adventure of taking Christ where he had never been preached before – it was all a memory. Now I was face to face with the reality of a people thankless and resistant to the message of the gospel, a harsh and inhospitable climate, a life isolated from other believers, depending solely on my personal relationship with God, and less than encouraging prospects, judging by the experience of the few missionaries who lived in these parts with very few visible results for their years of dedicated and faithful service.

We started to pray. What can you pray in a place like that? Almost the only valid prayer is, 'Lord, send workers to this town. Lord, raise up messengers ready to give their lives so that this town can hear your gospel.' One of the group prayed this prayer aloud, and at that moment a struggle began inside my heart, the like of which I have seldom known. I resisted saying 'Amen', because I knew that to pray like that without being prepared to be the answer to my own prayer was the utmost hypocrisy. 'Here I am, Lord, send him.' It's the equivalent of the non-Christian's swearing – we see a situation which upsets and frustrates us, or where we feel unable to do anything, and since we can't let out more than a gentle 'oh flip', we pray to God and our consciences are somewhat eased. But it generally doesn't mean any more than that.

I felt a bit like that. I was on the edge of tears, not over the condition of this insignificant town, but over the hardness of my own heart. I continued struggling, like Jacob with the angel, until finally, more than a week later, I was able to let go of my life into my loving Father's hands and say I was ready to do his will. Now I could pray, now I could ask God to send workers to this town, left behind a few days ago on our journey, and to other towns we had come across during that time. 'Lord, send someone here. If you want me to go, here I am. If not me, Lord, raise up someone else.'

I have never been back to that town, and I would have difficulty finding it today, over 20 years later. But I give thanks to God for teaching me there what it meant to pray; more than that, what it meant to intercede.

We are approaching the end of our look at this subject. Ezekiel 22:30–31 is in my opinion one of the saddest verses of the whole Bible. In it God shares with us his desire not to have to pour out his wrath on the earth, if only there were someone who would intervene as Moses did, and Aaron, and the Lord Jesus.

> I looked for a man among them who would build up the wall and stand before me in the gap on behalf of the land so that I would not have to destroy it, *but I found none*. So I will pour out my wrath on them and consume them with my fiery anger, bringing down on their own heads all they have done. (Italics mine)

How tragic. But even more tragically, this story keeps on repeating itself today. We who know the heart of our God, who have the testimony of the Scriptures and the clear commandment of the Lord Jesus to take his gospel to the ends of the earth, carry on turning a blind eye to the reality of nations, towns and peoples who don't know Christ, while God is seeking someone who will stand in the gap before him on their behalf. For how long will we close our hearts? For how long will we refuse to share this ministry with him? There are thousands and thousands of peoples, races, cities, countries, who have no one to bring them before God like this. And God is trusting in us, his people, redeemed to be kings and priests on the earth, so that he does not have to pour out his justified wrath on them.

Will you accept the challenge to be an intercessor?

4

Did You Know. . .

. . .that the name 'Jehovah' does not appear in the Holy
Scriptures? It is used frequently in the English King James
Version and the Living Bible. In spite of its common use
among evangelicals in Spanish-speaking countries owing to
its inclusion in the Reina-Valera translation, the most popular Hispanic version, it does not appear in the original
Hebrew. We have found something else in our Bibles that is
not inspired by God.

The name of God is present in its original form in the Old
Testament. It is written with four Hebrew letters thus: יהוה,
which transliterates as 'YHWH' or 'Yahweh', known to
theologians as the 'tetragrammaton' (a word which means
nothing more than 'four letters'. Isn't it amazing how theology can bewilder us with mere terminology?). However,
out of respect for the name of God, or perhaps for fear of
falling into the sin of blasphemy (taking the Lord's name in
vain), the Jews had ceased to pronounce this name long
before the time of Jesus. In its place they usually used
'Adonai', which means 'Lord'.

As we have already seen, the Hebrew text was written

without using vowels. Later on the Masoretes added in vowels to facilitate reading, and put the vowels of 'Adonai' together with the consonants of 'Yahweh'. Although 'YHWH' appeared in the text, when reading aloud 'Adonai' had to be spoken, and the vowels served as a reminder. No Jew would ever think of combining the two forms, using the vowels from 'Adonai' with the consonants of 'YHWH' – that would have been unthinkable. (For those who are interested in the actual Hebrew, we have explained this process in more detail at the end of the chapter.)

Unfortunately, Christians in general didn't know this, and after a while it occurred to a Spanish monk, at the end of the thirteenth century, to make this impossible combination, resulting more or less in 'Jahovah', the form later popularised as the English word 'Jehovah'. (This is the earliest known use of the word, published in the book *Pugeo Fidei* by the monk Raymundus Martini in 1270.) But it is a word that simply *cannot* exist. It is as ridiculous as writing the name of the city of Liverpool using just the consonants (LVRPL), and then combining this with the vowels from Manchester. Who ever heard of the famous city of 'Laverpel'? The following quotes confirm the truth of this:

• Jehovah is a Christian transcription of the tetragrammaton widely accepted by many Christians as the authentic reproduction of the sacred name of God in Hebrew, but now recognised as a later hybrid form never used by the Jews. (*Webster's Third New International Dictionary*)
• Jehovah: an erroneous form of the name of the God of Israel. (*American Encyclopaedia*)
• Jehovah: An erroneous reproduction of the name of the God of Israel. The error arose among Christians in the Middle Ages

when the consonants YHVH (JHVH) were combined with the vowels of ADONAI. . . (*Encyclopaedia Britannica*)

- Jehovah, false form of the divine name Yave. (*New Catholic Encyclopaedia*)
- Jehovah is an incorrect pronunciation of the Hebrew YHWH , the name of God. This pronunciation is grammatically impossible. The form 'Jehovah' is a philological impossibility. (*The Jewish Encyclopaedia*)
- YHWH. The personal name of the God of Israel is written in the Hebrew Bible with the four consonants 'YHWH' and is known as the 'tetragrammaton'. Up until at least the destruction of the First Temple in the year 586 BC, this name was regularly pronounced with its appropriate vowels, as can be seen in the letters of Lachish, written shortly before this date . . . When erudite Christians from Europe began to study Hebrew they did not understand the real significance of this, and introduced the hybrid name 'Jehovah'. . . (*Judaic Encyclopaedia*)
- [Jehovah] is an artificial form. (*The Interpreter's Bible Dictionary*)
- The vowels from one word with the consonants from another were erroneously read as Jehovah. (*International Encyclopaedia*)
- Jehovah: is an incorrect reconstruction of the name of God in the Old Testament. (*Merit's Student Encyclopaedia*)

Well, it does seem to be incorrect, doesn't it? So how should the name be translated and used in our Bibles? There are a number of options. The original form 'YHWH' could simply be left as it is, and readers be allowed to decide for themselves how they want to pronounce it, but this is not a serious solution for a Bible which aims to be accessible to a modern population. A 'translation' of the *sense* of the biblical name could be sought, such as in the French Louis Segond Bible, where *L'Éternel* ('the Eternal') is used to express the meaning of 'I am that I am' and 'I will be who I will be' contained in the Hebrew original from which the name is derived. Or we could adopt the solution of the Jewish people and put 'Lord', just as they did in their Greek translation of the Scriptures. It seems that the Bible itself approves of this last option, since God allowed the replacement of 'YHWH' with *kurios* ('Lord') in Greek, in the quotes from the Old Testament which appear in the New.

Well, now we have learned something else. Perhaps we will even be able to correct the supposed 'Jehovah's Witnesses' who knock on our doors. But at the end of the day it is not just knowledge of the true *name* of God that counts – it is knowing *him*, receiving that revelation of his nature in the depth of our being, and being able to name him not just 'Saviour' of our lives, but also 'Lord'. May he truly be our Lord, may his authority rule in our lives, and may we be ready to obey him as Lord. In this way I am sure that the kingdom of God will advance with greater speed and the day will draw closer when at 'the name of Jesus all beings in heaven, on earth, and in the world below will fall on their knees, and all will openly proclaim that Jesus Christ is Lord, to the glory of God the Father' (Philippians 2:10–11 GNB).

*   *   *

Here is a more detailed explanation of the process by which the name of 'Jehovah' was reached.

יהוה   These are the four consonants of the name of God in Hebrew (YHWH).

אדני   This is the word 'Adonai', or 'Lord', in Hebrew, without vowel pointing.

אֲדֹנָי   With the inclusion of the vowels, this is what the final form of 'Adonai' looks like in Hebrew. Note the dots below and above the letters which are vowels.

יְהֹוָה   These vowels were inserted between the consonants of 'יהוה' to remind the reader not to pronounce it, but to say 'Adonai'. This is the form which appears in the Hebrew Bible today, and which gave rise to the totally incorrect pronunciation of 'Jehovah'.

5

A Fine Little Number – What Verses Have to Do with Women

C harles Marsh, a former missionary in Chad, Central Africa, tells of a startling incident which occurred at the entrance to a humble chapel in a rural area of that country. It was a normal Pentecostal church, small but fervent, whose congregation loved and worshipped God with all their hearts. The meeting had already started when a young woman approached the gap in the wall which served as a doorway into the simple building. She was dressed in the traditional *panya* of that part of Africa, a simple strip of brightly coloured cloth, around two metres long and one metre wide, worn wound around the body at the waist, or breasts if the wearer is not breast-feeding a child, as was the case with this young woman.

She stopped at the doorway and, without further ado, took the cloth from around her body, folded it carefully before placing it on her head, and entered the church completely naked, but with her head covered. She took her seat among the other women as the meeting continued, without anyone being distracted from their worship of God. In this church, had a woman entered without wearing anything on her head it would have caused a scandal, but the lack of any other clothes . . . didn't matter at all.

The role of women in the church has always been a subject of debate, discord and division. Questions such as the use of head-coverings, the contribution of women in public meetings and the limits on women's ministries have filled innumerable books and, if something doesn't change in the evangelical world, will continue to be discussed for several years to come. I do not purport here to give 'the definitive solution' to the question, not by any means, but rather to contribute to the debate, within the limits of the central line of thought of this book.

Because, as we have seen, not everything in our Bibles is inspired. The divisions we usually find in our contemporary editions, such as the chapters, do not form part of the inspired text. Neither do the verses. But at the end of the day it's not so difficult to decide to ignore that big number which separates two chapters, and carry on reading, thus following the original thought of the author.

It is a little bit more difficult with the verses. While chapters, as we saw earlier, saw their origin over a period of many centuries, the verses owe their existence to the perceived necessity of making smaller divisions within the long chapters which had already been adopted. These verses were published for the first time in the text of the Greek New Testament in 1551, and in the English Bible from 1557 onwards. The Geneva Bible, which appeared in 1560, was the first to carry both chapters and verses.

Although they are very useful for identifying and localising specific texts, the verses contribute to our difficulties in understanding the message of the Bible in two fundamental ways. Let's see how.

1 In the first place, the most natural way to read a text is in sentences,

2 these being contained in paragraphs which unite the thoughts of the author.

3 It is not normal,

4 nor does it help us,

5 when the continuity of the text is broken up by little numbers,

6 although the main problem is not due to the little numbers,

7 but to the custom traditionally employed in some Bible editions of starting every new verse on a new line.

8 Why is it necessary to start a new line just because it's a new 'verse',

9 especially when this occurs in the middle of a sentence?

10 It does nothing to clarify the meaning of the sentence. On the contrary, in fact, it only serves

11 to break the flow of the most natural reading of the passage,

12 doesn't it?

In the second place, apart from breaking the continuity of the text, the actual thought of a text is then divided into separate blocks which govern our understanding of the contents, sometimes dividing in places that do not correspond to those allowed for in the original Greek text. Thankfully, however, most modern Bible editions group the verses into paragraphs, allowing for a much more natural reading.

Who decided how the text was to be divided up into

verses? Most point to Robert Estienne, or Stephanus in
Latin, as the 'inventor' of these divisions. This Parisian editor and printer published various editions of the New Testament in Greek and Latin. His fourth edition, published in
1551, contained the Greek text divided up into verses for
the first time, along with Erasmus's translation into Latin
and Hieronimus's 'Vulgate' version. This was the edition
which came to be known as the *Textus Receptus*, the
'received' version. Although it should not be considered a
100 per cent reliable text, it was used as the basic text for
most translations until the appearance of 'critical' editions,
which were constructed from evidence from earlier manuscripts. (Various parts of the Greek text of the book of Revelation, for example, were back-translated from the Latin,
because Stephanus did not have any Greek manuscripts
that contained those verses.)

Just how did he decide where to place those divisions
into verses? Well, I don't know the true story, but I do like
to imagine this erudite itinerant printer of the sixteenth
century making the most of the time he spent travelling
about on his donkey by studying the Scriptures and
defining the verses to be used in his new edition of the Bible
that was due to be published. The only thing was that now
and then his pen slipped up or down a bit as his donkey
stumbled on the road, and so a verse ended up in not quite
the right place. Is that just my imagination? No doubt it is,
although we do know that John Wesley travelled on horse-
back, reading in his saddle, and must have fallen off more
than once because he was paying more attention to his
books than to where he was going! And Stephanus's son
does in fact inform us that his father *did* undertake this

work whilst on a journey from Paris to Lyons, although he rather gives the impression that he did the work when they stopped in inns along the way. But however it came about, what is certain is that the division of the verses does not always correspond to the most natural, or the most appropriate, place. But what has all this got to do with women? Well, quite a lot actually. Let's look for a moment at Ephesians 5:21 – 6:9, a passage which speaks about relationships in Christian homes (including slaves and masters, husbands and wives, parents and children). How is this text usually read?

First we find a verse that speaks about mutual submission. Full stop, new line. Next verse. Some Bibles even put a division here between this section and the previous one, but *after* verse 21, thus joining verse 21 – with its note on mutual submission – to the other comments on the Christian life contained in that previous section. We continue reading, almost as if we were starting a completely new topic, about interpersonal relations in the family home. It is introduced with these words: 'Wives, submit to your husbands as to the Lord.' However, a careful reading of these verses in the original text rules out the division of ideas suggested, and offers us a different perspective on the role of women and the meaning of their submission.

Translated literally from the Greek, verses 21 and 22 read thus: 'Submitting yourselves one to another in reverence to Christ, the women to their own husbands as to the Lord. . .' As we can see, according to the most accurate texts, the phrase beginning 'wives' (or 'women') does not contain its own verb, but is utterly dependent on the verb in the previous sentence. These two verses cannot be separated and put into two different blocks, much less paragraphs, because the original Greek simply does not allow it. They should be read together. Even if translated like this, for example, 'Submit to one another out of reverence for Christ; wives, submit to your husbands. . .' the two verses should not be separated from each other.

It is a command to mutual submission, in which a wife has a special responsibility towards her husband, but which makes no sense if the obligation of the believing husband also to be submitted to his wife is excluded. The passage gives some specific guidelines for each member of the Christian household (or each Christian member of a non-Christian household), but all within the general context of submission to one another. Focusing on the submission of the woman, without explaining in what sense her husband is also submitted to her, takes this command out of its context and results in unbalanced beliefs and practices.

Here I should explain a couple of things. First of all, we are talking about a reading of the Greek according to the best texts. To be fair to some of the older translations, it should be mentioned that the *Textus Receptus*, the Greek text which formed the basis for them, does include a verb in the second half of the phrase. This was the text they had in the sixteenth century, but obviously it didn't incorporate the evidence of much older and better quality texts which were discovered later. I do not want to enter too much into a critical analysis of the original texts, but it *is* clear that the second verb was included in an attempt to clarify the meaning of the sentence in texts which were copied much later on. In all probability, it did *not* appear in the original text.

In the second place, we need to correct some wrong

thinking which, although ruled out by this and other similar texts in the Bible, still prevails in the Lord's church. The text is talking about husbands and wives, not men and women. It does not attempt to legislate on relationships between the sexes in general, but in the family or, rather, between spouses. The aim of the passage is to protect the social equilibrium of the home. It applies Christian freedom to this basic institution of society and thus is directed, as we have already noted, at husbands and wives, parents and children, slaves and masters. (Our concept of slavery does not correspond 100 per cent to the reality of the ancient Greek and Roman world either. Although there were cases of maltreatment and abuse, of course, in most cases the slaves formed part of the household and in many cases were treated as members of the family. This is why they are included in this section, since a slave was normally a member of a household.)

Paul is not talking at the level of society, or of the church, but of the family. He is laying a foundation for Christian living in the home, and it is a hermeneutical error of great magnitude to apply this passage, or similar ones like 1 Corinthians 14:33–35, to women in general. The relationship between husband and wife, God's established order for the family, is one thing, and the relationship between men and women in the church, or in society – including, of course, single women – is something completely different.

Let's think for a moment. Does this passage forbid a slave to be named as the leader of a congregation, as long as he is qualified according to the biblical requirements? And if his master is also there? Could a slave therefore have authority over his master as far as the church was concerned?

Let's consider another example. Lydia is married to John. She is a business school graduate, while he left school at 16 to work as a bank clerk. Years later, she is offered the job of manager at the very same branch where her husband works. Can she accept the position? Can she have authority over her husband in this context? Should he submit to her as far as the guidelines and norms of the bank are concerned? Does this contradict biblical teaching?

And what happens at the level of the church? Should women always be 'in submission' to the men there? And what does 'in submission' mean? What should we do if 10 women are converted in a town, and no men? After a few years of training, learning to use the Word of God, discovering their gifts, suddenly a man is converted, one of their husbands. Praise the Lord! But what happens now? Should he assume immediate leadership of the group simply because he is a man? Could he receive discipleship, leadership, or Bible teaching from one of the mature women of the group? Or even from his own wife?

The Bible, in spite of being written at a time when women, as a rule, occupied a very inferior position to men, does allow the ministry of women in a wide range of expressions. Although infrequent, the presence of these women who clearly occupied positions of authority and had important ministries demonstrates that there was no ban on the participation of women at these levels, even if their 'inferior' position and their lack of preparation, education and opportunities tended to exclude them from leadership or spiritual ministries.

Deborah was a 'judge'; that is, leader of the whole of Israel. There was no higher position in the society of that time. Miriam, Aaron and Moses' sister, and Huldah, were prophetesses. The four unmarried daughters of Philip prophesied, and there was provision for those women who wanted to speak prophetically in the church in Corinth.

Phoebe was a deaconess, although the text tells us that she was a 'deacon', using the masculine term in the Greek. This seems to indicate that the use of masculine terms can include both men and women, which has wide implications for our understanding of the offices and ministries mentioned in the New Testament. It is said of Phoebe that she was 'a great help' to many people, translating the Greek word *prostatis*, which is used only once in the New Testament. In the literature of the time it refers to a 'patroness', a woman who had authority over others, who guarded and protected them, caring for them out of her own resources. It is derived from the verb *proistemi*, which only Paul uses in the New Testament, a total of eight times, and always with the meaning of 'preside' or 'govern' (Romans 12:8; 1 Thessalonians 5:12; 1 Timothy 3:4–5, 12; 5:17; Titus 3:8, 14). It is also used several times in the Greek translation of the Old Testament, the Septuagint (or LXX), again usually with the meaning of a head of household or leader. It seems that Phoebe did rather more than 'help' the brothers in Cenchrea.

Priscilla certainly taught Apollos, and by the way in which Paul refers to the couple as 'Priscilla and Aquila', putting the name of the wife before that of her husband, it seems that she had the lion's share of the ministry of teaching and leading the church which met in their house. Timothy also received instruction in the Scriptures from his mother and grandmother, and it looks as if they did a pretty good job with him. In the book of Revelation, the church in Thyatira is not reprimanded for having a woman leader, nor for being prepared to listen to the prophecies and teaching of a woman, but for tolerating her false doctrine. She had even been offered the opportunity to repent – again, not of having dared to teach or prophesy, nor of having authority in that church, but of what she was teaching.

It is not possible here to deal in depth with the various interpretations of 1 Timothy 2:11–12, and ample literature is available on the subject elsewhere. But a couple of points must be made. First, this text – often along with 1 Corinthians 14:33–35 – is usually quoted as the *sine qua non* on the subject by those who have already made up their minds on the issue of women in leadership. It tends to be presented as the only point of discussion, being both the starting point and conclusion of the argument, the 'trump card' that defeats all other contrary ideas. However, it is rarely taken against the backdrop of the testimony of the whole of Scripture, nor alongside a genuine historical investigation into the kind of roles that women actually did exercise during the period in which Paul was writing. The interpretation of one verse (and especially one in such a difficult context – what do you think verse 15 means?) should not be made to contradict what is clearly expressed in the general context of the whole biblical canon and the testimony of early church history. Such an approach sheds much light on this verse.

Secondly, this is the *only* passage in Scripture that explicitly limits the role of women in teaching. Given the commendation that Paul gives elsewhere to women co-workers, some of whom (such as Priscilla) were undoubtedly involved in teaching, it is understandable that this text is difficult to interpret correctly. However, a huge hermeneutical leap is involved if we choose to take this one text, ignoring the specific context in which it was given and the long-term solution to the problem that Paul proposes, and extend it to a blanket prohibition on women's involvement in leadership roles or teaching activity. Paul is addressing the issue of the Ephesian women's general lack of education, and justifiably will not allow them to take authority in the church. Let them be educated first, and the same applies in many parts of the world today. His appeal to creation order parallels his comments in 1 Corinthians 11 on the wearing of head-coverings – an application which is accepted by most today as being culturally conditioned – and cannot be seen as an expression of the 'fundamental order of things' for humanity, male and female, for all time.

And finally on this text, perhaps we should just emphasise that it would be tragic if a dubious interpretation of one verse made us discount the evidence of the real ministry of women in the biblical narrative and condemn more than 60 per cent of the body of Christ today to the fringes. There are other interpretations which harmonise with the general tenor of the Bible, and which allow women to use the gifts God has given them. A narrow interpretation of this text which leads us to judge a woman's potential gifts and ministry on the basis of her gender, rather than by the growing fruit of a life under the guidance of the Holy Spirit and the training of the church, calls into question our own capacity as leaders and mature interpreters of God's Word. The church is much poorer as a result.

It is said that Jesus only chose men to be apostles. This is true, but it is also true that he only chose free Jewish men. No slaves, and no Gentiles. But we don't for that reason exclude non-Jews and slaves (if there are any these days, in our Western nations at least) from being able to exercise ministries in the church. And, in fact, after the Twelve, other apostles were chosen. We should not confuse the two terms: one is used to designate the men who formed Jesus' 'special' group during his earthly ministry, and the other came to mean 'missionary', referring to those who had the ministry of starting new work. Barnabas, for example, was considered an apostle.

Anyway, amongst the apostles we also find in Romans 16:7 Andronicus and Junia. (That's how it's written in the AV at least, using the woman's name 'Junia', although the NIV puts 'Junias' here, as if it were a man's name. The NLT, whilst using the woman's name, is the most honest in giving a footnote which says that either is in fact permissible.) That Andronicus was a man, this much is clear, but who was Junia(s)? Was this person a man or a woman? I don't want to confuse readers by entering into details about the conjugation of Greek nouns, but I must at least point out that, grammatically, it could be either masculine or feminine. Both 'Junia' (woman) and 'Junias' (man) are translations which in theory would be possible.

However, the masculine name Junias is unknown in Greek literature of the period – it simply does not exist as a real name. It seems that no one was actually called Junias. But, on the other hand, we find that the female form, Junia, was common and exists in both Greek and Latin. In any other context there would be no room for argument – it would be Junia, a woman. Some manuscripts even read

'Julia' here, using a name that was exclusively a woman's name, having confused the two. It seems, then, that Paul was talking about a couple, and that he considered them apostles. Whatever, we can see that it was accepted that a woman could be considered an apostle without any problem.

Romans 16:6 also mentions a certain Mary, who 'worked very hard for you', and verses 12 and 13 refer to another three women who 'worked very hard in the Lord'. Paul mentions two other women in a different place who, together with their male co-workers, 'contended at my side' (Philippians 4:3). Were they really only making the tea and sweeping the floor after the meeting?

I could continue in this vein, but I would rather refer readers to other books to find out more on the subject. What type of ministry is implied by these texts? The Scriptures offer women ample opportunities to develop their gifts on a par with men and to be involved in ministry together with them. Are we going to limit women in their desire to serve God with the abilities that he has given them because of mistaken ideas about submission?

This interpretative error becomes most patent in the area of missions. Whether we like to admit it or not, the greatest advances in world evangelisation are due to the involvement of women, the vast majority of them single. Seeing themselves deprived of opportunities to exercise their gifts, to express through Christian service their love for the Lord, many have turned their gaze towards the nations, to dedicate themselves to the work of evangelism and ministry there.

And the same men who systematically deny them the opportunity to preach, teach and lead in their home churches, praise God for their efforts and allow them to do 'out there' what they could never dream of doing in their country of origin. There they can pastor, teach, disciple and organise the churches that are born as fruit of their work. There they have authority over men, disciples whom they train and lead, and the work grows and is blessed. They lay their hands on young pastors to impart spiritual gifts, and in all of this do the work which in their own countries is reserved for the men.

This relegation of women to a secondary position is the product, of course, of many social, historical and spiritual factors. A wrong reading of Ephesians 5:21–22, owing in part to the badly placed division of two verses, has contributed to the creation and propagation of a position which discriminates against women, both in the sphere of the church and in society in general, which has been influenced over the centuries by the position of the church. It is up to us to seek an impartial reading of the Scriptures, with the inspired message they do contain, and correct the abuses and errors of the past.

The church today is in a position to throw off the yoke of discrimination which has dogged us since the Garden of Eden and face with unstoppable energy the challenge of world evangelisation in the twenty-first century. Releasing the creative, dynamic abilities of the women in our churches, permitting them to occupy the ministries for which the Lord has created and saved them, we will make significant advances in the task of taking the gospel of the kingdom to all the nations, and hasten the day when our Lord Jesus returns in glory. So be it. Come, Lord Jesus.

6

The Most Surprising Verse in the Bible

It was so difficult for him to understand my decision. His grandson, after qualifying in his profession and getting himself a good job, was going to throw it all overboard in response to the call of God to serve him among the nations. Even at the time I was converted my grandfather had trouble understanding it. I was English, therefore I was already a believer, wasn't I? Why did I need to 'get converted'? As I had come to know Christ in Paris, he presumed at first that I'd become a Catholic, probably under the influence of some French girl. But now what was happening to his grandson?

I tried, as gently as I could, to explain my decision to him, how privileged I felt serving God, and the example of the life of the Lord Jesus. 'But look what you're leaving behind: your career, your profession, your future. . .' he insisted.

'Yes,' I replied, 'but just think what Jesus left behind to save us. Having seen what he did, what I'm doing doesn't seem all that much.'

'That may be,' he said, very seriously, his face showing how difficult it was for him to cope with the crazy ideas of his grandson. I was dumbfounded when he added, 'But you're a teacher, you've got a job with a future – he was only a carpenter.'

'He was only a carpenter.' That was not exactly what I'd had in mind when I referred to all that the Lord Jesus had left behind to demonstrate his love for us. . . I was actually thinking of the glories of heaven, his relationship with the Father, everything that it meant to be God. That he emptied himself, taking on the nature of a servant, being born as a man, to be obedient to death on a cross – and all because of his love for me. Amazing! Sometimes we forget the cost of his commitment to save us. Sometimes, too, we forget what it costs us to be faithful to him, to want to be his co-workers in the expansion of his kingdom here on earth. And what's more, sometimes our version of the Bible does not help us to remember.

We have already seen that neither the chapters nor the verses are inspired by God. They have not always been put in the most appropriate places. But these are not the only divisions in the Bible. The biblical text as it is presented in our Bibles is usually divided not only by those little, or not so little, numbers, but also into distinct sections headed with subtitles, put there undoubtedly with the intention of clarifying the meaning to the reader and helping us to follow what we are reading. Normally they mark the start of a new paragraph, or a section comprising a number of paragraphs, and so they aim to guide us in our study.

The paragraph is, without a doubt, the basic unit for understanding any text. It contains the different elements which together make up the line of thought of the author and constitute his message. It is the only division inherent in a biblical text, since it reflects the original thought taking shape on the page. The Bible should be studied fundamentally at the level of paragraphs rather than words, verses or, it goes without saying, chapters.

I am sure that the editors of our Bibles make every effort to discover these natural divisions in the text, and to give them a subtitle which describes as exactly as possible the central theme. But they don't always get it right. Or rather, they don't always agree, and they can't all be right. A quick comparison of various Bibles will reveal these differences. It might simply be that it is difficult to divide up the line of thought of the author – especially with Paul, with his 'sentences' which frequently stretch for dozens of lines. Or elsewhere it might be the Greek grammar itself which does not lend itself to a division in the most natural place.

Let's get to the interesting bit. There are also times when, even though there is agreement (more or less) on the correct point of division, the imposition of a subtitle hides the connections between paragraphs which are the key to understanding the progression of the argument. It can break the continuity of the author's thought, and we lose something of his message. This is what happens in the first chapter of Colossians.

After the greeting and Paul's prayer for the believers in Colossae, Paul starts telling us about Christ. In most Bibles this is the beginning of a new section entitled, for example, 'The Supremacy of Christ' (NIV), or 'The Person and Work of Christ' (GNB). Colossians 1:15–23 is indeed a majestic exposition of the person of Christ and his work of redemption and reconciliation for the benefit of humanity. It puts Christ above all created beings, as the only Creator and the visible image of the invisible God, reminding us of the words of John in his Gospel: 'No-one has ever seen God, but God the One and Only, who is at the Father's side, has made him known,' and, 'Anyone who has seen me has seen the Father' (John 1:18; 14:9). Jesus Christ is the one who reigns over all creation, but he also came and lived among us, and even died to become the first to rise again and so guarantee the resurrection of all those who believe in him.

That's right – he did not stay up there in heaven; he came down, so that the Father could reconcile all things to himself, this entire created universe, through him. By means of his blood poured out on the cross he made peace with us, those who have responded to his call and have received him. We who used to be 'far away from God and were his enemies', in other words utter wretches of the first order, have now been reconciled to the God whom we had rejected. We can present ourselves as holy, without blemish and blameless before him, continuing faithfully in this message of the gospel which we have received.

How did we come into all these benefits? What was the price that was paid so that we could enjoy the freedom in which we live today? 'By means of the physical death of his Son' (Colossians 1:22 GNB), or, to put it another way, 'by Christ's physical body through death' (NIV). These are not the theoretical words of a theologian, a 'spiritual' commentary on a mystical and sublime act. It is talking about a real life, a cruel death, a body of flesh and blood, with nerves which took the messages of pain to a living brain. It is talking about a body like yours and mine, a body of 'flesh', consciously given over to physical suffering which only ended with the slow death of crucifixion.

Contrary to the doctrine of the Gnostics, Jesus *did* come in a real human body. 'The Word became flesh' (John 1:14), the eternal Son of God, the Word which created the whole world, then became part of that world by taking on a body of flesh. It was his *body* which was anointed for burial (Mark 14:8). When we break bread, we remember his *body* given for us (Luke 22:19). And according to Peter, 'He himself bore our sins in his *body* on the tree' (1 Peter 2:24). The Antichrist is whoever denies that Jesus Christ has come 'in the flesh' (1 John 4:2–3). We stand before a historical act, lived out in the body of the very Son of God incarnate.

Conscious of how Jesus suffered to win our salvation, let's follow the apostle's line of thought. In most of our Bibles this is difficult, because verse 24 marks the start of a new 'section' entitled 'Paul's Labour for the Church' (NIV), 'Paul's Work as a Servant of the Church' (GNB), or something of that kind. In reality it is difficult to break up the text here. In verse 23, for example, speaking about this gospel preached throughout the world, Paul has already announced himself as minister. Why break the thread of his message? But our Bibles do so, and we lose the real link between the description of Jesus as Saviour and Redeemer, and our own commitment as ministers of Christ.

Let's reconnect with the central theme of Colossians 1:15–23 (that is, the redemption of God's creation, achieved by the suffering of Christ in his body of flesh) and continue reading in verse 24, ignoring the subtitle which has been inserted there. We find what appears to be one of the most surprising verses in the whole Bible: 'And now I am happy about my sufferings for you, for by means of my physical sufferings I am helping to complete what still remains of

Christ's sufferings on behalf of his body, the church' (GNB).
Or, as the NIV puts it, 'I fill up in my flesh what is still lacking in regard to Christ's afflictions.'

Can anything be 'lacking' from the sufferings of Christ?
Didn't he do a complete work on the cross? How can we
claim to be 'filling up' this lack? Is more suffering really necessary for the church, his body, to be made perfect? How
can me suffering help anyone else to be saved? Isn't this a
doctrine of 'salvation by works'? Doesn't that sound rather
'Catholic'? These and a hundred other questions rush into
our minds when we consider this verse, and I'm quite sure
that, if it wasn't in the Bible, more than one of us would
consider it heretical.

But there it is. The advance of the gospel in the world is
based upon the suffering already paid by the Lord Jesus in
his own body on the cross, *and* the afflictions of those of us
who follow him, paying a real price in our bodies so that his
message reaches the whole of creation. Our flesh, our body,
is involved in this work in the same way that he also
involved his body, his flesh.

Our redemption came through the offering of the physical body of Jesus, and continues today through the same
surrendering of his body, which is the church, you and me.
There is a price to be paid if the redemption of the universal church of Christ is to be carried through to the end. If
that were not the case, don't you think the world would
have been reached centuries ago? In addition to the unique
price of the blood of the Lord Jesus Christ poured out once
for all, the work of revealing the bride of Christ still needs
the surrender of his body, the church.

There is nothing lacking from the redemptive work of

Christ. It is impossible to add even the tiniest bit to what Christ completed on Calvary. When he said, 'It is finished,' he had offered his own life as a sacrifice to the Father for our sins, and nothing else was necessary to ensure our salvation, our redemption from the power of the devil. Nothing! He did not need to suffer any more, and we cannot add anything to his work by our sufferings. It is a complete work, finished, written indelibly with his own blood in the volumes of human history.

However, as members of his body it now falls to us to continue this suffering, this surrender to the will of our Father, whatever the consequences might be for our lives. It is not a suffering which produces salvation, in the sense that nothing can be added to the finished work of Jesus, but it is a necessary suffering if the message of redemption is to be preached and demonstrated as true throughout the nations of the world. And Christ so identifies with his church that he calls it his own body, and feels its sufferings as if they were his own. Didn't the resurrected Christ say to Paul, at that time known as Saul, 'Saul, Saul, why do you persecute me?' The persecution let loose against the church was against the Lord himself, and the sufferings of the faithful were his own.

In one scene from the book of Revelation, we see 'under the altar the souls of those who had been slain because of the word of God and the testimony they had maintained' (Revelation 6:9). They were asking, understandably, how much time was left until the end of all things, when their blood would be avenged. (So we are not the only ones who want to know when the end of the world will come – it seems that even the dead have a keen interest in eschatology.)

When will it be? They are not told, but have to wait a little while longer 'until the number of their fellow-servants and brothers who were to be killed as they had been was completed' (Revelation 6:11).

Most of the apostles paid the ultimate price for being Christ's witnesses. And even before his death, the biography of Paul reveals his many sufferings, which he greeted with joy, knowing his purpose within God's plan. 'We always carry around in our body the death of Jesus,' he tells us, but he is able to stand firm because he knows why this is necessary: 'so that the life of Jesus may also be revealed in our body . . . So then, death is at work in us, but life is at work in you' (2 Corinthians 4:10, 12).

Did he not feel this suffering? What are 2 Corinthians 4:7–12 and 6:4–10 telling us, if not of the physical consequences of commitment to God and his will in the life of Paul? He wasn't 'floating around', anaesthetised to suffering and need, but he considered them of no importance compared with the privilege of taking the message of salvation to others. 'When you pass through the waters, I will be with you' (Isaiah 43:2). God will be with us, but we need to pass through the waters. Surrendering our lives is something very real, tangible, lived out day by day in our feelings of pain and frustration, but carried through by the power of God.

Some years later, approaching the end of his earthly career, the apostle was able to write to the Philippians with the same desire he had always had 'so that now as always, Christ will be exalted in my body, whether by life or by death' (Philippians 1:20). This poor body which had borne beating after beating in the service of Christ is being offered to God afresh on the altar of obedience.

As it was then, so today the gospel will never reach the resistant peoples of the 10/40 window if there are no 'bodies' to take it there. Yes, these days a lot can be done by radio, internet, television and other communications media, but nothing takes the place of a human being, surrendered at the feet of Jesus to live out his will. Affirming 'I'm with you in spirit' will never advance the cause of the gospel as much as being there in body and soul. (To tell you the truth, I don't really fancy the idea of having human spirits floating around with me, but hey, that's another subject.)

What better example could we have than the Lord Jesus himself? In his prophetic interpretation of Psalm 40 the author of the letter to the Hebrews says this: 'When Christ was about to come into the world, he said to God: "You do not want sacrifices and offerings, but you have prepared a body for me."' Then, with this physical body which God had given him, he offers himself in God's service: 'Here I am, to do your will, O God, just as it is written of me in the book of the Law' (Hebrews 10:5–7 GNB).

God has also prepared a body for us. He wrote about us in a book, and not only our names in the book of life, but also these good works which he has prepared in advance for us to do (see Ephesians 2:10). In his eyes no sacrifice, no offering, has any value compared with the surrender of our bodies for his service. We can do nothing better than offer our whole lives, encapsulated in this body, to do his will.

God has a will for our lives – a good, pleasing and perfect will. But God does not reveal this will to those who are merely curious; he reveals it to those who desire to obey. Paul invites us to 'know', or, even better, 'experience' or

'test' what the will of God is for our lives. This is not a theoretical knowledge, as if we had arrived at the conclusion of
what God wants for our lives and now we have to decide
whether we want it or not. It is the *experience* of living in the
will of God, expressed day by day in our lives. Perhaps we will
never understand it, but we can live it and experience it.

To do this we are asked to 'present [our] bodies as living
sacrifices, holy and pleasing to God' (Romans 12:1–2). Not
our spirits, nor our souls, but our *bodies*. At the end of the
day, where our bodies go the rest of us has to follow. I am
asked to present to him my body, as a living sacrifice – not
a sacrifice performed only once with a knife upon an altar,
which in all probability would be easier, but a *living*
sacrifice, moment by moment, dead to myself and alive to
God.

Of course, our bodies are already his. We were bought
with a price, our bodies are members of Christ and temples
of the Holy Spirit (see 1 Corinthians 6:14–20). The tense of
the verb in Romans 12 – an aorist which indicates a finished
action at one point in time – is asking us to present our body
to God once for all, not offer it to him every now and then,
as if it had escaped out of his hands. No, our body belongs
to him, and to use it for ends which are not part of his will
is to steal and abuse what does not belong to us any more.

However, we *can* confirm the fact that we belong to him,
and that we want our bodies to remain his. That they are
available to do his will, a will which is carried out in the
evangelisation of the world. A will in which some of us will
only find the purpose for our lives serving him among the
nations. A will which is waiting for the surrender of bodies
prepared to obey him, whatever the cost.

'Lord, you know that you have my mouth to speak your words to a world which needs you. You have my arms to embrace the outcasts and rejected, and to communicate your love. My ears to listen, to understand others, and show them that they are important. My eyes to weep with those who weep and express your love in the way I look at them. My hands to comfort the broken-hearted. My feet to take me to the place where you want me to serve. My brain to master new languages, and my tongue to communicate you wherever you want to send me. Lord, here I am, send me.'

If the world is going to hear the gospel and see that it is a credible and trustworthy message, the price that the church will have to pay is a real price and will not go unnoticed. You will feel it in your body. In the same way that salvation has been won for us 'by Christ's physical body through death', so also this salvation will be preached and believed in the world as we 'fill up in [our] flesh what is still lacking in regard to Christ's afflictions, for the sake of his body, which is the church'.

7

The Parable of the Soils

It had only taken us a few hours to drive down from the high mountain pass, where eagles soared over rugged crags, and we now found ourselves in a small town on the edge of the largest desert in the world. It was a town like any other on the Saharan side of the Atlas mountains. A signpost read 'Timbuktu – 53 camel days', but I didn't want to go quite that far. It turned out that the day we arrived was the day for the *souk*, the weekly market that served as a meeting place for the hamlets round about and gave them the chance to buy and sell their wares. By mid-morning the town square was filled with the hubbub of noises, voices, shouts, smells and the non-stop hustle and bustle that characterises such places on these days.

While the group I was with set about exploring the old town centre, I wandered haphazardly around that crowded square, finally stopping next to one of the countless stalls, if that's what they can be called. Because I was a foreigner, they always tried to sell me something at ten times its real value, but buying things no longer held that much attraction for me and I had learned how to say 'no' without offending anyone. In fact, after the customary greetings, that day I started to joke with the jewellery seller with whom I had struck up a kind of conversation.

'How much will you give me for this box? Six hundred *reals*?' I asked him, quoting a price in the country's previous currency which older people still used to work out prices. 'For you, *sadiqi* [my friend], cheap, good price. How much can you pay? It's good quality, solid silver. . .'

The 'tourist guide' had become the salesman, and was attempting to sell the craftsman his own product. Smiling from ear to ear, he took me by the hand and sat me down at his side under the shade of the canvas that protected him from the hot desert sun. I very soon had a new friend, and together we drank a refreshing glass of mint tea. We chatted for a good while about everything and nothing, and unhurriedly watched the crowd go by, getting on with their lives amidst the ever-present clouds of dust.

In this relaxed atmosphere I got out my 'parable box', a simple shoebox covered with gold paper, but which never failed to captivate onlookers. 'What on earth has he got there?' When all is said and done, it was nothing more than a few simple drawings, cardboard figures, and all kinds of accessories to enable me to tell a basic story visually, without feeling so limited by my still impoverished knowledge of the language. It was little more than a three-dimensional flannelgraph, but it did the job, and how!

With the solemnity that a story-teller is supposed to have, little by little I produced from this Pandora's box a whole series of objects that would illustrate the parable I was about to narrate: a green cloth, which I always used as a background; another piece of cloth which would become a 'field', drawings, grains of wheat, bits of plants, stones, little birds, a blazing sun, and who knows what else. Suddenly, the field was replaced by a human heart, and the story was repeated, while the crowd of onlookers who had gathered nodded their approval with a whole host of gestures and words of affirmation. I like to think that the first time this story was told, almost 2,000 years ago, it happened in a similar place, with similar people, to whom the living example of the growth of seeds in a field communicated the truths of the kingdom of God.

I resisted the temptation to tell another story, and sat down again with the one who had already become my sponsor, who started to ask me about the story. How could he also produce this good fruit? His heart was also full of thistles, but could the ground be cleared? Could he give God a good harvest? I don't know how this man's personal pilgrimage finished, but that day at least he understood something of the eternal gospel, and he set himself to seek God. When I later said goodbye, we were able to pray together to the One who was able and willing to plough the hardened ground of his heart, asking him to sow his precious word there and protect it until it bore fruit. I only hope that it did indeed fall into good soil.

Oh yes, the parable of the sower. What a wonderful piece of teaching. It has served as raw material for countless sermons throughout the history of the church, and quite rightly so. It is found in the three synoptic Gospels and, in my Bible at least, it is simply entitled 'The Parable of the Sower'.

But let's stop to think for a minute. We have already seen that the division of the text into paragraphs is decided by the publisher of a particular version, and that these divisions do not form part of the inspired text. The same applies to any subtitles which may be used, and we must thus understand that the words 'The Parable of the Sower' do not form part of the original text. None of the 'titles' that we find in our Bibles are there in the originals (with the exception of the titles to the majority of the psalms, which are in fact generally the first verse of the Hebrew text). If you want to check this out, you simply need to have a look at two different Bibles. The titles are not all the same, and sometimes they are even found in different places, according to the editor's better judgement. They have been placed in our editions of the Bible and offer us a division into paragraphs or sections that undoubtedly help us to read more coherently. But they are not inspired by God.

However, as they are there at the start of a passage, they do tend to condition our thinking when we come to read and interpret what follows. And they are not always the most appropriate title. For example, the parable of the 'Prodigal Son' is not really about a prodigal son. (And while we are on the subject, how many of us actually know the real meaning of 'prodigal'? It does not mean 'lost' or 'wayward', but rather 'wasteful of one's means', 'squandering', or 'spendthrift'.) Instead, the parable is really about the 'prodigious father' – the love, goodness, understanding and forgiveness of a father who had been rejected, insulted and dishonoured, all in an overwhelming manner if we take into consideration the social customs of that time. The important thing is not what the lost son may or may not have done, but rather how the father receives him, in a way that would be totally inconceivable to the story's first audience.

What is more, to focus on the 'prodigal son' causes us to lose sight of the older son, who is also one of the story's central characters. Jesus finishes this teaching on the goodness and compassion of God with a telling criticism of his own people who, like the older son, looked askance at the mercy which was shown to the 'unacceptable': to sinners, to the 'unclean', and to Gentiles. Israel had always been with God, and should not now resent the incorporation of those who had lived far from him.

And what about the parable of the sower? Is it really about 'the sower'? In one sense it is, because the sower is there in the story. But in another sense it isn't, because the main point of the story has nothing to do with the person of the sower, as it also has nothing to do with the seed. The sower is the same each time he goes out to sow, being none other than the Son of God himself. And the seed represents the Word of God, the message of salvation. What changes is the nature of the ground in which the seed is sown, and that is where we find the message that Jesus was wanting to get over. It is simply about the difference between distinct soils. In the same way as the results of sowing depend on the quality of the land into which seed is sown, and the circumstances in which the seed has to grow, we cannot and should not expect the same results in different situations. This would not be natural, and Jesus warns us that life simply is not like that. Why not change the title in your Bible, and write in something like 'The Parable of the Soils'?

With the main point of this parable in mind, we can now proceed to give it a more adequate interpretation, one which is missed by the majority of readers. Our 'traditional' understanding suggests simply that when the Word is

THE PARABLE OF THE SOILS

preached, we can expect that some people will reject our message, that others will accept it but will not last for various reasons, and that only a minority will get to produce long-lasting and permanent fruit. However, there are two other aspects that we need to consider.

First, when we interpret the parables, we rarely take into account the real-life situation in which Jesus was giving his teaching. Every parable has a real background, an event or a question which served as a backdrop for the teaching that was given. The parables were not given in a 'void', as anecdotes deprived of a context and able to be applied to any circumstance that might take our fancy today. They must be placed in this 'real' context. What is more, the 'literary' context must also be taken into account, the place that the author chooses to assign to the parable, because it contributes to the development of his narrative of the life and ministry of the Lord Jesus.

When we examine these contexts, we find that Jesus told this parable at a decisive moment in his ministry, particularly in the process of the training of the disciples. He had already spent considerable time preaching around the towns, making known 'the gospel of the kingdom', a task in which his followers were actively involved. His fame went before him, and he was experiencing ever greater confrontations with the nation's political and religious leaders. Furthermore, from the crowd who accompanied him he had appointed 12 as apostles, leaders-in-training for the future Christian community.

It was the time to invest heavily in them. There is a time to scatter the precious seed all over everywhere, sowing generously with our lives. But there is also a time to stop sowing 'randomly' and to invest our resources in those who will produce fruit. And now Jesus was planning to give himself more and more to his own disciples, preparing them for the time when he would be taken from them. The 'parable of the soils' explains and announces the change in priorities which was going to take place in his ministry. Having sown along paths, amongst thorns and in rocky soil, now he was to concentrate on those who had shown themselves to be 'good soil' and who, 'with a noble and good heart . . . by persevering', would produce a good crop.

Secondly, we must allow the central focus of the parable itself to condition our main interpretation. The parable looks at different *soils* and how the eternal and immutable Word of God, sown by the Son of Man himself, is received in each of them. It draws our attention to the fact that the success of sowing does not depend so much on the quality of the seed or the capability of the sower, but rather on the very nature of the place which is sown. Yes, it is true, there really are places which are 'hard' or resistant to the gospel, and others which are more 'receptive'.

Many missionaries from Latin-American countries, who are used to seeing 'instant' results, despair very easily when they run up against the apparent hardness of people in Western Europe or parts of the Muslim world. 'What's wrong with me?' they ask themselves, heads hung low. They left their homes with experience of work that had been carried out well, souls saved, churches planted, meeting places built. Filled with faith and hope, and not a few dreams about 'conquering' towns for Christ, they moved out into the 'mission field' in obedience to the Lord's call and with 'faith aims' for their future ministries. And now, working there with the same determination, with prayer, fasting and dedication, they use all possible means to bring people to Christ and build his church. But no one is converted – or maybe just a few, and mostly social outcasts at that – and they begin to ask themselves why.

'Where's the problem?' the anxious missionaries ask. And the conclusion many reach is that they themselves are the root of the problem. Perhaps they have lost something of their faith, or perhaps they aren't praying with sufficient dedication, they think. They'll just have to work harder, pray more, and more intensely, because things just can't go on like this. . . Little by little, even though they continue praying and working harder than ever, the absence of 'results' grips their soul and they lose even the little faith they had left. They continue with the external signs of their ministry, but are completely defeated inside.

But what about the church who sent them? Do they show understanding for their missionary's situation? Do they realise that the spiritual realities of Venice, Islamabad, Athens, Rabat, Vienna, Dacca, Madrid or Bamako are not those of Rio de Janeiro, Buenos Aires or Lima? Or that Mozambique and Macedonia present two very different kinds of challenge? Unfortunately, it must be pointed out that churches who understand these things are very few and far between. In a very short space of time the missions board or the church itself is 'demanding' results from its missionaries.

The missionaries were sent out on a wave of emotion and fervour. They are the representatives of the church to penetrate into the darkest places with the light of the gospel. They are taking the victory of Christ, and nothing and no one will be able to stop them. At their farewell service encouraging remarks and 'prophetic words' combined to guarantee their immediate success, and all eyes are on them as they set off to 'the mission field'.

Along with this spiritual expectation goes the matter of the church's economic investment. After all, the missionary is 'paid' by the church, and they want to see a good 'return' on their investment. Supporting a young person overseas involves a heavy financial commitment, often equal to the salary of a pastor along with his family 'at home', and in the case of missionary families the investment required spirals upwards.

Even taking all this into account, it seems that the past has been forgotten. That past when other churches in other nations invested so that foreign missionaries could dedicate themselves to the work of evangelisation and church plant-ing, often working for years without seeing spectacular results. That past when people were not converted so 'eas-ily', when each soul represented a victory that was won with great effort, and when churches were small and weak. But our memory is short, and today we demand from our missionaries an unrealistic 'yield'. If the churches of the first missionaries who worked in Latin America had demanded the same from them, it is highly unlikely that many would have lasted more than one 'term' and that the spectacular growth of recent years would ever have been obtained.

With this 'forgetfulness', and the desire to see its own denomination planted in far-off lands, the missionary is being asked to do the impossible. 'How many churches have you planted?' they are asked after a few months, or perhaps one short year. The poor missionary has not even had time to learn the language yet, not to mention adapt to a different culture in which he feels like a fish out of water. But this matters little to a congregation bent on 'success', and members already start to talk about this missionary's 'failure', comparing him behind his back with other more 'fruitful' workers in other fields. All of this goes on, of course, without the grumblers knowing the reality of the field in which the missionary is ministering. The church becomes police, witness, judge and jury to these workers, all in a hearing convened in their absence, and they are then condemned to the ignominy of wearing the label of 'failure' for the rest of their lives.

The worst thing about all this is that the missionaries know what is going on. They were brought up there, and know how people speak about those who do not produce immediate and impressive results. They are conscious of what is expected of them, and do not want to disappoint. Their bulletins and prayer letters become more and more 'evangelastic', with phrases which are as deceptive as they are inaccurate, such as 'many responded to the Lord', 'the work is growing', or 'the Lord's blessing went with us at every step of the campaign'.

Unfortunately, under this kind of pressure some even get to the point where 'exaggeration' (in other words, 'poetic licence' or supposedly 'white' lies) becomes lying plain and simple, and all sorts of figures are invented, along with photos of congresses or others' churches, all so as not to fall into disgrace with the sending church. In this way, little by little, they condemn themselves to living in unreality and thus seal their own premature departure from the field. Our own self-esteem will not allow us to live submerged in this type of fantasy world for very long. So, soon they return to their countries of origin, labelling as 'missionary cemeteries' countries such as Spain, Austria, Italy, Tunisia, etc.

Am I exaggerating? Perhaps, but not very much. All that has been written here is based on real cases, whose essential elements have been repeated all too often. What is saddest is that all these scenes could have been avoided had the 'parable of the soils' been taken into account. But it seems that some of us think ourselves to be wiser than the Lord himself, and we do not want to accept that things are like that. We are not prepared to pay the price for effective preparation of the harder lands, investing in sowing without seeing an immediate and abundant harvest. And we carry on labelling as 'failure' any lack of results similar to those which currently characterise work in our own countries.

This is why the long-term success of mission work is totally dependent on the church receiving and taking to heart an adequate programme of education in missions. Each member must understand the reality of the field to which their missionaries have been sent. Their workers need the understanding of those who support them, so that they will not be judged before time on the basis of the 'results' they obtain, and so that they can be totally honest with the church without losing their support. It is only a church which is informed and genuinely conscious of the specific situation in which their workers find themselves that can act in this way.

Beyond this, the training process of the missionaries themselves must prepare them to be able to adapt their expectations of results to the specific field of work. It must provide them with the kind of emotional strength that will enable them to experience results which are 'poor' when compared to what they have achieved in previous years in their own countries, without entering into self-condemnation, and without losing heart about their call or their own capabilities for the ministry. In other words, it must prepare them for a completely different reality.

(It is perhaps worthwhile pointing out here that few really believe that things will be like this until they find themselves bashing their own heads against a brick wall as they experience it all first hand. I have seen it countless times. On explaining to candidates that 'Spain is different', I can see the look of disbelief in their eyes. I can speak until I am blue in the face, and even though they don't say anything, it is obvious that inside they simply will not accept what I am saying. It won't be like that for *them*. *They* know how to fast and pray until they see breakthrough, and *they* will be able to overcome the spiritual opposition and see decisive victories. It may be that all other pastors and missionaries have not been able to do this – they obviously must have a very impoverished spiritual life – but *they* certainly will. . . I have to remind each one of them: 'You are not the first missionary, nor the last, nor the best.' And then it's just a matter of aiming to be around, at their side, as they start to wake up to the painful reality that I was, in fact, right all along. If they last two years, and really do adapt, they generally end up doing an excellent job.)

The 'parable of the soils' portrays to us one important aspect of missions in today's world. Workers are still needed in those less receptive places, but workers who understand things as they really are, and who are prepared to pay the price of a long-term ministry, sowing with their own lives. And those who send missionaries, those who support in prayer and with their resources, must be humble realists, so that the words Jesus spoke to the Pharisees should not also be applied to them: 'They tie up heavy loads and put them on men's shoulders, but they themselves are not willing to lift a finger to move them' (Matthew 23:4).

Let us allow the Lord Jesus' simple teaching on the different soils to penetrate into our hearts and change our expectations. Let us quit judging according to purely human criteria, and accept the spiritual realities of the world that God communicates to us in his Word. In this way, with God's help, perhaps we will be a little more able to take on the task of preaching the gospel of the kingdom in the whole world with greater perseverance and understanding. By God's grace may it be so.

8

'The Woman You Put Here with Me'

He was a sweet, pleasant chap, and very committed to the Lord's work. In fact, he was studying at Bible school to be able to serve as a pastor. Born in Sicily, he had spent most of his life in France, but held on to a great many of his Mediterranean, Latin roots.

I don't remember how the conversation came about, or how he came to be taking part in it, but we started talking about women, *le donne*. And not just women, but women in the church. Quite a subject. Suddenly his girlfriend, a young woman with a concept of the role of women which went somewhat beyond the classic *cucina, chièsa, letto* ('kitchen, church, bed') which for the most part still characterised the conservative society of Mediterranean Italy, shouted at him, 'How dare you!'

It seems that this Sicilian – sweet, but chauvinistic – believed that the soul of a man was worth more to God than that of a woman. That was the bottom line: if God had to choose between saving a man or a woman, the man would win every time. (That must be why our evangelical churches are full of so many more men than women, then. . .) Of course, when pressed to justify this rather unorthodox belief, he couldn't, and had to retire with his Mediterranean male honour a little bruised. But I don't think he will have changed his opinion that easily; attitudes acquired over a whole lifetime are not thrown overboard just like that.

Let's get back to talking about women. They have been scapegoats for failure-conscious men ever since Adam pointed to Eve and put the blame on her, effectively blaming God himself: 'The woman *you* put here with me. . .' A stumbling block to the poor devout man whose only goal in life is to be a 'good Christian', women have come to be seen as the root of all evil – along with money, of course. Together with the desire for power, these three are known as the worst enemies of the spiritual man, the insidious 'three "f"s': finance, fame and females.

The apostle Paul himself confirms this image of the *femme fatale*, the dangerous woman, doesn't he? Reading the historical interpretations offered on some of his most debated texts, it is not surprising that he has been branded a misogynist by the main body of those who speak up for women's rights. Doesn't he say, 'It is good for a man not to touch a woman' (1 Corinthians 7:1 AV)? (And by 'touch', we know he is not referring to an accidental brush, or a light stroke of the hand. . .) He might as well have said, 'Avoid them as far as possible, including your own wife if you happen to be unfortunate enough to have one. It's much better for you. . .'

And if that were not enough, he concludes this section of his letter to the unruly Corinthians by giving some advice to those who have not yet passed through the gates of matrimony. Doesn't he say that he would prefer everyone to be like him (that is, or so they tell us, single)? If the one who decides to marry 'his virgin' does right, the one who decides not to marry her (or give her in marriage) does even better (1 Corinthians 7:36–38 – and there's a text that needs some serious, thorough exegesis). In summary, if you can't control yourself, well, in that case (and only in that case) get married. Poor man, consumed by sexual desires that you ought to have been able to control by now; it's better to marry than to burn with passion (v. 9), but much better to throw cold water on your passion and extinguish it as quickly as possible. But if, despite everything, having struggled fiercely against those evil desires, you are still prisoner to the attractions of the female body (although, to be fair, it's not their fault that they look that way – that's how God made them), then there's no way round it – to the altar with you!

This vision of 'chastity', of the supremacy and spirituality of celibacy, together with a conviction of the intrinsic evil of sexual relations, has dominated in the body of Christ almost since its beginning. Living in a church plagued by the Greek philosophical concept of the dichotomy of body and soul, very few people throughout history have been able to give balanced and biblical teaching on human sexuality. Origen, for example, castrated himself in his zeal for Christ – though whether this was to curb his own inflamed desire, or to render powerless alleged criticism of his contact with women disciples, we will perhaps never know. The pseudepigraphal work 'The Acts of Thomas' describes *marital* sexual union as a 'deed of shame', a 'partnership of corruption' and 'filthy intercourse'. And Augustine, whose writings have influenced the development of Western theology more than any other, saw in his own struggles with sexual lust a reflection of man's original sin. We live with that legacy today.

The Corinthians also suffered these effects of Greek philosophy, which exalted the spirit or soul at the expense of the poor body that binds the spirit to its terrestrial home and hinders believers in their spiritual walk. As Plato said, *soma sema*; that is, 'body = prison': the body is the prison of the soul, which will find its true freedom only after death, when finally it is freed from its shell of revolting flesh. Until then, during our earthly pilgrimage we have to fight constantly against the bad influences of our weak and loathsome bodies. Let's repeat several times in Orwellian manner, 'Spirit good – body bad; spirit good – body bad,' and I am sure we will find that we come to believe it too.

All this has very little to do with the biblical concept of humanity, but it has dominated Christian thinking for many years, and even today shows little sign of dying out. But God created humanity good – body, soul and spirit. There is not the slightest suggestion in the Word of God that Adam and Eve's physical being was any less perfect than their spirit. And when they fell, the whole lot fell, not just the body. Sin does not have its origin, nor even its dwelling place, in the body – it is equally at home both in the human soul (in anger or jealousy, for example) and in the spirit (as is the case with idolatry or occult practices). Paul's technical use of the word 'flesh' whenever he refers to the sinful nature has caused many to identify the body as the seat of sin, an understandable error in light of the erroneous concepts which have become ingrained over centuries.

And what about heaven? Platonic thinking is light years

away from the Judaeo-Christian hope of bodily resurrection as the reward of the righteous, and not the 'freeing' of
the spirit. Heaven will not be home to a host of disembod-
ied spirits, but of whole people, enjoying a new, eternal
body that God has prepared for us, in the new heavens *and*
the new earth. Our experience will not be one of being
freed from the body, but one of being freed from the 'flesh';
that is, the sinful sickness which infects our whole being
and embitters all our present efforts to reach the perfection
of our heavenly Father.

But the Corinthian believers did not just suffer from this
perversion of human reality. They had also adopted the
norms of the majority of Roman religious expressions,
which accentuated liturgy, ritual and ceremony above the
essential or experiential content of worship. The important
thing was not your intention to worship God, or the condition of your heart, but precisely *what* you did. And consequently holiness had to do with forms rather than deeds, a
purity which was ceremonial rather than moral.

Thus, with a concept of purity which was basically ceremonial, and with their world view dominated by this mistaken understanding of the physical part of man and,
therefore, of his sexuality, it is not surprising that they did
not want to 'touch' their own wives. They imagined that it
was impossible to please God if they carried with them into
his presence the 'filth' of a recent 'unclean' contact. Thus
influenced, they even reached the point of wanting to separate from their unbelieving spouses, for fear of 'contamination'. That is why Paul exhorts them regarding the
possibility of the partner being 'sanctified' through them.
He is not making a case for 'salvation by proxy', a thing

which does not exist (despite the affirmations to the contrary by the Mormons, who get baptised on behalf of their deceased loved ones). Rather, he is talking about a purely ceremonial cleanness.

With this we arrive at our theme – that not everything in our Bibles is inspired. We have already looked at the chapters, the verses, the paragraphs; now it's time to look at the punctuation. We have seen that the biblical manuscripts were written without any punctuation at all. This does not mean that the reality which these signs represent for us was not present in the mind of the writer, rather simply that they were never put down on the page. Of course he knew what he wanted to say – it's just that *we* don't. However, we have no alternative but to insert punctuation into our Bibles, since today no one would understand anything without it. It is not normally cause for any dispute. The problem arises on those occasions when the meaning of the original is not 100 per cent clear, and we have no option but to impose upon the text punctuation which limits the possible meaning of a phrase.

There were no exclamation or question marks, for example. (We are referring to the 'autographs', or original manuscripts; of course question marks were used later on, and as such appear in the Greek texts we have today in the form of a semicolon: ';'.) So, do Jesus' words in John 16:31 form a question or an affirmation? Should it read 'Do you believe?' or 'You *do* believe!'? Finding the right point to mark the beginning of a sentence can also be complicated. What do you do with Ephesians 1:3–14, for example, since in the Greek it consists of one single phrase? Hence we find different sentence divisions in different translations.

Neither are there 'speech marks' to define the beginning
and end of a verbal or textual quotation. Usually the parti-
cle *hoti*, or 'that', is used to indicate the beginning of a spoken quote. But where does it end? The most famous verse
in the Bible, for example, John 3:16, is found part way
through one of Jesus' speeches, which begins in verse 10.
But where does the speech finish and John's commentary
start? After verse 17? Verse 21? Or even just after verse 16
itself? The NIV ends the quotation after verse 21, as does the
Spanish Reina-Valera version of 1995, while the AV, along
with the Reina-Valera of 1960, the 'bulwark' of the Hispanic Protestant Bibles, does not commit itself – it simply
does not put any indication at all and leaves the decision
freely to the inclination of the reader. Don't let a 'red-letter
Bible' fool you – no one knows where Jesus actually
stopped speaking.

We could say the same for Paul's speech which he relates
to us in Galatians 2. He rebukes Peter for his hypocrisy in
verse 14, but when does he stop? Some interpreters put the
inverted commas to mark the end of his little sermon right
after verse 14, others after verse 16, and others extend it up
to verse 21. Who is right? There are opinions to suit all
tastes. There's no way of knowing, and indeed all punctuation found in the Bible has been put there by the decision
of the editors.

You probably think I'm going off the point slightly, but
that's not the case, as we shall now see.

When Paul wrote his first letter to the Corinthians, he
was not acting on revelations and words of knowledge that
he had received from the Lord. Someone in the church had
written to him (sneak!) to share their worries about the

state of the congregation, and to make a few comments and ask a few questions of a doctrinal and ethical nature. Let's look at 6:12–13, for example. Does Paul really say, 'Everything is permissible,' and, 'Food for the stomach and the stomach for food'? Isn't it more accurate to do as the NIV does and put these statements in inverted commas to show that Paul is quoting from the original letter which he had received from the Corinthians? Or, as it reads in the GNB, 'Someone will say, "I am allowed to do anything" . . . Someone else will say, "Food is for the stomach, and the stomach is for food"' – adding the words 'someone [else] will say' and the speech marks to clarify the most probable meaning.

In chapter 7 Paul goes on specifically and deliberately to answer the questions and comments which had been made by the Corinthians. 'Now for the matters you wrote about' introduces the next phrase, which surely contains the first thing about which they had written: 'It is good for a man not to have sexual relations with a woman' (1 Corinthians 7:1, my translation). Does this phrase express Paul's own thoughts? As he himself would say, 'By no means!' Rather, it is a quotation from their letter to him, and he answers them firmly. A paraphrase could express it like this: 'Let's look now at what you wrote to me about: "It is good for a man not to sleep with a woman." But because of the danger of sexual immorality, it's better for everyone to have their own wife or husband. . .'

This famous phrase, then, is wrongly attributed to Paul, simply because original manuscripts do not contain punctuation. It does not express Paul's opinion, rather the opposite, and is soundly corrected by him. Having made that clear, he then proceeds to demolish the pretensions of the Corinthians with simple but clear teaching about the naturalness of marriage, and sexual relations as a fundamental part of it. Paul does not accept the alternative which they propose to marriage, a celibacy which is apparently spiritual but which makes them vulnerable to the temptations of sexual immorality.

And what an amazing concept of women Paul had. Here there is not the slightest trace of misogyny. Since when in the Greek and Roman world did a woman have sexual rights? She was the receptacle of the man's seed, the object of his pleasure and not much else. Only a woman of dubious reputation would have a desire for sexual relations. Is it possible for women to have good sexual desires? But Paul is not interested in this caricature of the woman as created by God, and he raises her to the level of her husband. The husband's body belongs to his wife, and he does not have the right to deny her sexual pleasure, however spiritual this chastity might appear. To call a spade a spade, women's sexual rights take priority over men's delusions of spiritual grandeur.

Neither does the fear of contamination give him the right to offer to God what legitimately belongs to another, in this case his wife, as the Pharisees used to do with their cries of *korban*, dedicating to God what he had asked them to give to their parents. Paul opens only a very narrow door for sexual abstinence, so that both believers can dedicate themselves to prayer, and this only for a limited time and by mutual agreement. She has as much say in the regulation of their sexual life as he does. Even in his role as 'head of the family' God does not give the man the right to take this decision without the express agreement of his wife. And we dare to call Paul a misogynist. . .

These surprising declarations become even more incredible when set against the backdrop of the reality of the Hebrew mindset of the first century, especially that of the Pharisees among whom Paul had received his education. 'Praise be to you, Lord of heaven and earth, for not making me a Gentile,' they used to pray, continuing: 'Praise be to you . . . for not making me a woman.' The poor women had to content themselves with a commendable 'Thank you for having made me what I am', a prayer which in reality is much closer to the heart of the gospel.

Sorry, but women are not an easy target onto which men can discharge their own spiritual failures. They are not the lowest of the low, nor the incurable root of our difficulties. Male and female God created us, and he designed us for each other. We must work to restore to women the dignity inherent in their creation in the *imago dei*, and rid ourselves of the corrupt and perverted mentalities that pollute our guilt-laden concepts of sexuality.

In short, it is definitely good for a man to 'touch' a woman, as long as she's his wife!

9

'Do You Truly Love Me
More than These?'

It was one of those grey days that are so characteristic of England: the sky was grey, the city looked grey through the falling drizzle, and I felt even more grey, if that were possible. Sitting on a swing in the children's play park, I poured out my heart to God, and my tears onto the already wet ground.

I could not believe it. Only three months earlier we had begun 'going out together', a decision taken just before the summer holidays at the university where we were studying. They had been three months without much contact apart from a short visit and periodic letters and the occasional phone call while I was working abroad. We saw each other again, and she told me that she did not know if she believed in God any more, that she had lost her faith.

Now what? Lord, why? She knew that I did not want to get involved with a girl who was not a Christian, and she gave me complete freedom to abandon our relationship. Now it was up to me, and I found myself at a crossroads from which there could only be one way out, but it hurt. Did I have a choice? Yes, I did, although in reality it was no choice at all. Would I relegate my love for the God who saved me to second place? Would I permit a human love to separate me from him who had said so unmistakably that he who loved father, mother, son or daughter more than him was not worthy to be his disciple?

Hours later I pulled myself out of the hole of self-pity in which I was wallowing and set off home. The afternoon remained shrouded in tones of grey which dominated the city, but in my heart there were clear blue skies. I could not deny the evident sadness I felt, but now it did not hurt quite so much. I had responded to the gentle but persistent voice of my Lord which said, 'Neil, do you truly love me? Do you love me more than her?' That day I got to know my own heart a little better. A few priorities had been established in my life, and I knew it. 'Yes, Lord, you know I love you.'

I am sure that I am not the only one who has passed through that storm of confused emotions, resulting in a renewed commitment to God and a real and tangible peace. Almost 2,000 years before, another of the Lord's disciples went through circumstances quite different from mine, but with the same results: a deeper love for his Lord and a commitment to serve God wherever he wanted to send him.

Yes, Peter. Spokesman of the disciples, 'big mouth', simple fisherman called to be a fisher of men, once again he had put his foot in it. 'Even if all fall away, I will not . . . Even if I have to die with you, I will never disown you' (Mark 14:29, 31). Open mouth, insert foot. Yes, I know, all the rest said the same, but it was Peter who had led the way, and were they going to be outdone by him? They all agreed that they would never abandon the Lord Jesus even if they had to die with him. And then they all, with one accord, ran away to save their skins. Just when he needed them, they abandoned him, and he was left completely alone.

Peter, however, did not just abandon him together with the rest. He followed 'at a safe distance' and was there, watching Jesus and watched by him, but without declaring himself to be with him. On the contrary, he denied him, he denied him again, and finally he swore with curses that he did not know him, the strongest way to declare the truth of something, calling upon God as witness of the truth of his affirmation. I don't know which is worse, but I think I would prefer to be left alone than to watch with my own eyes the conclusive denial of one of those who ought to have been by my side. That's being left doubly alone.

Oh, Peter. Impetuous as an adolescent, brave for a moment but paralysed by fear minutes later. Quick to speak, but without the stability of character necessary to be faithful to his own words. In one blink of an eye his whole world collapsed. What must that look from the Lord have been like, which in that instant penetrated to the depths of Peter's soul and sent him running outside to weep bitterly over the poverty of his heart? Full of love, without doubt, but a love which reveals our neediness and confronts us with our pitiful reality.

So Peter entered the most acute crisis he had ever experienced. Not even those words, 'Get behind me, Satan,' which Jesus had levelled at him a few months earlier had opened his heart like that look. What was happening? Had he really denied him? How was it possible? What an imbecile, what a coward he had been. Full of self-reproach, and almost certainly with a good dose of self-pity, Peter sank into a depression which he probably imagined he would never come out of. But God had other plans for him.

I don't think Peter could see much further than his own tears and the darkness of his heart, broken by the recognition of his own personal failure. But Jesus, the first and the last, the beginning and the end, who examines our hearts and our inner being, knew his disciple and had already predicted not only his fall but also his repentant return, and his consequent responsibility as a servant of God: 'Simon, Simon, Satan has asked to sift you as wheat. But I have prayed for you, Simon, that your faith may not fail. And when you have turned back, strengthen your brothers' (Luke 22:32–33). They all abandoned the Lord, Peter included, but once restored from this experience he would be the key figure in the consolation of his brothers and the building up of this first Christian community.

The process of formation through which God puts his servants is no theoretical training, from which they graduate with a diploma in their hand, their heads full of more or less useful information, and an institutional status which commands the respect of their future victims. It is a process of formation primarily of the person, of the character. We are human beings, not human 'doings', and God is much more interested in what we are than in what we can do. Our theology schools would do well to take note of that. When he moulds us for his service, his priority is what we become, not what we know or learn to do. And failure plays a fundamental role in this process.

Peter had already been told that he would become a fisher of men, but not even he had imagined what this transformation would imply. At that moment he cannot even think about fishing for men. He has failed. He has let God down. His dreams and ambitions of sharing the glory of his Messiah in the coming kingdom are shattered, and he can see no future. Jesus won't be counting on him any more, obviously. He is deeply disappointed in himself, and sure that it is impossible for him to be any use now.

Yes, the Lord has risen from the dead, and Peter does not doubt the victory of his Lord over the powers of death and hell. He has seen the Lord, is convinced of his identity and his authority, but Jesus' resurrection does not take away the shame of his own failure. He remains submerged in the living memory of that horrible night, when he was unable to overcome his cowardice and denied his Redeemer, Saviour and Friend, in front of his very eyes. Nothing, no, nothing, would ever be able to erase this memory. He was a man condemned to live under the shadow of his own inadequacy.

From this desperate perspective it is understandable why Peter should go back to his old job. The fisherman goes back to fishing, convinced that he will never be any use again fishing for men. 'I'm going fishing,' he tells the other disciples, with no further explanation, and they decide to go with him (John 21:3 GNB). He had always been the first one, the pioneer, the leader of leaders, and he was still. For good or for bad, Peter found himself out in front. A long, fruitless night awaited them, and in the tiredness of a night of hard labour, having caught absolutely nothing, a scene more sensitive and yet thrilling than the ending of any romantic comedy was being prepared. But before we see the final act, let's take a small interval to set the scene for the unfolding of this drama.

All this is very nice, it's true, but what does it have to do with our theme? We have already seen that some parts of our Bibles do not form part of the original, inspired texts. However, if we are honest we will have to admit that not even the actual words in our Bibles are inspired. They are translated, more or less accurately, from the words found in the original Greek, Hebrew and Aramaic texts.

There is never an *exact* equivalence between two words in different languages. The 'sphere of reference' of a Spanish word, for example, never overlaps 100 per cent with an English word, and vice versa. One single word can be translated by various words in another language, and any one of those has a much wider meaning than the word originally translated, and would need more words again to express its meaning in the first language. This language thing is complicated, and it is obvious that God did a good job at Babel.

Hebrew is a very poetic language, and sometimes imprecise, with many words whose meaning today is somewhat obscure. In contrast, Greek is ideal for philosophical expression, with a less 'florid' vocabulary, but with some very precise verbal constructions. Our translations try hard to get as close as possible to the meaning of the inspired original, usually with great success. However, there are occasions when this lack of 'equivalence' between the vocabulary, grammar or idiomatic expression of Greek, Aramaic, Hebrew and English makes an exact expression of the fullness of the original impossible. The translator has no choice but to use an expression which best represents the sense of the original, and to put a footnote at the bottom of the page to clarify the meaning if he considers it necessary or useful.

There are two main verbs in biblical Greek which are

translated in English as 'to love'. They have similar meanings, but only similar, yet they are both contained within the sphere of reference of 'to love' in English. They do not refer to the same type of love. One, *agapao*, refers mainly to the perfect love God has for us, or an equivalent love that we have for another person, a love which loves without thinking about what it will receive in return.

Let's coin a new word in English for this one, 'to agapay'. (There is no reason why we shouldn't do this if we want to. 'Baptism' is basically a Greek word written with English letters, as are 'bishop', 'angel' and 'apostle'. Whenever there is a gap in our native vocabulary, 'importing' words is the most common solution. In England we play the piano, eat pretzels and yoghurt, and drink tea, whilst in France during *le weekend* many young people listen to *le walkman*. So maybe we should start aiming to agapay one another as God agapayed us.) This term is found in scriptures such as this: 'For God so "agapayed" the world that he gave his one and only Son.' Or again, 'A new commandment I give you, that you "agapay" one another as I have "agapayed" you.' This verb is a derivative of the well-known term *agape*, which refers to this same type of love.

But then we have the term *phileo*, which means to love in the sense of fondness, friendship, appreciation, esteem; to love as a friend. It is the love of relationships, reciprocal love, more than giving love. The 'philosopher' is the friend of *sophia*, wisdom. 'Philadelphia' speaks of love between brothers, and 'Theophilus' is one who loves God.

Having made this foray into the territory of the original biblical languages, let's go back to Peter and his exhausted companions in the boat on the Sea of Galilee. Suddenly a mysterious figure appears on the shore and tells them to throw their nets overboard one last time. Immediately the nets fill up with fish, and the echo of a past experience rises up within Peter. 'It's the Lord!' John says to him (John 21:7). And Peter, who this time does not try walking on the water, gets dressed, throws himself into the water and swims the 100 metres to the shore to be with his Master, who once again has shown that he is Lord even of his profession. The fisherman was being fished again.

What was Peter thinking about? Perhaps he was remembering that time three years before, approximately, when for the first time Peter had found himself confronted with the reality of who Jesus was and who he himself was. After another night of fishing with no success he had lent his boat to Jesus for a while, so that Jesus could preach to the multitude from it. Once he had finished, Jesus had invited them to throw their nets out again. 'Who does this guy think he is?' Peter would have been thinking to himself. 'Well, just so he learns not to put his oar in where it doesn't belong. . .' Then he adds out loud, 'OK, Lord, whatever you say.'

But Jesus is Lord of all creation, as he would demonstrate to them fully on this very same Sea of Galilee at a future date. The nets filled up, and Peter was convicted in that instant of the true state of his heart. 'Go away from me, Lord; I am a sinful man!' Thank goodness the story does not end there. Jesus is not surprised by our stubbornness or our pride, nor by the complete list of our hidden sins which he already knows in detail. He had already seen what was inside Peter, and he still wanted him as a disciple, and more, as an instrument for his work. 'Don't be afraid; from now on you will catch men' (Luke 5:8–10).

An awareness of our complete inadequacy is closely linked with our possibility of being useful in the kingdom of God. Thus Peter's confession of inadequacy was immediately followed by a confirmation from the Lord that he would be used in his service. Like Isaiah of old, who, conscious of his sins, was called to take the Word of God to his nation, Peter heard the call of God to follow his Christ and be transformed into the central figure of the future community of the redeemed.

Now, with the events of recent months alive in his memory, Peter is confronted again with his failure as a disciple and the miraculous power of the Lord who had called him to his work. Why couldn't he just leave him alone? Having gone back to his old job, Peter found himself faced again with this Jesus, who would not let him forget so easily his calling to be a fisher of men.

After a leisurely breakfast on the beach, Jesus turns his gaze on Peter and asks him bluntly, 'Do you truly love me more than these?' In other words, 'Am I more important to you than this fishing business that you've gone back to?'

'Yes, Lord,' answers Peter, undoubtedly feeling a little uncomfortable, 'you know that I love you.'

'Feed my lambs,' replies Jesus, initiating the personalised process by which Peter would be restored to his calling and his responsibility in the early church (John 21:15).

Here we should take note of a difference which does not show up in the classic translation of the English-speaking world, the King James version (AV). Jesus has asked Peter, 'Do you agapay me?' In other words, 'Do you love me with all your heart, with a love which does not seek anything in return, a love that serves?' Peter, all too aware of his recent history, was unable to promise what he could not fulfil, and he knew he was not up to the demands being made. So he replied, 'Lord, you know that I phileo you.' In other words, 'You know that I love you as a friend, that I like you, but don't make me say something I can't live up to.' It is an important difference, as we shall see. The NIV at least tries to bring out this difference by using the expressions 'truly love' and 'love' to translate *agapao* and *phileo* respectively.

A second time Jesus asks him, 'Peter, do you truly love me, do you agapay me?'

Again Peter answers with painful honesty, 'You know that I love you, that I phileo you.'

And in spite of the evident lack in Peter's reply, Jesus continues restoring him: 'Take care of my sheep.'

However, the third time something has changed. 'Simon, son of John, do you love me? Do you phileo me?' Jesus has accepted that Peter cannot offer what he does not have, and he does not put any unrealistic conditions upon him in order to be able to follow his calling.

Peter is saddened to the depths of his heart, not because Jesus has asked him the same thing three times (which is what you would naturally think from reading this passage in the AV), but because this third time Jesus has come down to his level. It seems that Jesus is aware of the reality of his feeble commitment, and that Peter would not be able to carry on trying to 'be somebody' in Jesus' eyes.

'Lord,' says Peter, 'you know all things; you know that I love you, that I phileo you. I can't give you any more than that, and it hurts me to see you come down to my level. But yes, Lord, I love you as much as I can.'

'Feed my sheep.'

How amazing. Fully conscious of who he is, but now having lost his misplaced self-confidence, Peter listens to the renewal of his commission to serve God in the ministry. He can't believe it. How can Jesus depend on him, knowing what he is, and after what he has done? He is accepted just as he is and, what's more, he is useful just as he is. The recognition of his weakness was the decisive step needed to reach the goal he was after. It is no wonder that an ancient proverb tells us, 'It is better to win control over yourself than over whole cities' (Proverbs 16:32 GNB).

Nothing has changed today. The idea that you have to reach a level of mysterious spirituality in order to be able to serve God keeps many people from living a life useful for the kingdom. Jesus does not need us to be 'perfect' before we can respond to his call. The only thing he requires is that we are conscious of who we are, of his forgiveness and grace, and that we love him above everything else, even if our love is imperfect and doesn't measure up.

God does not ask the impossible of us. He knows that we are dust, and he wants us to know it too. He doesn't mind coming down to our level, and he accepts our many limitations, if we will only be sincere with him. His servants have always been humble people, more aware of their inadequacies than their abilities. What is our love for him? Isn't it in reality nothing more than the morning mist which disappears as the sun rises? If he had not loved us first, would we be capable of loving?

Now as then, Jesus is looking for men and women who are prepared to accept the challenge of allowing themselves to be moulded in his hands until they become fishers of men. It is neither an easy nor an instant process, and it involves the disciple in a journey of self-discovery which will lead to the edge of despair more than once. But it is worth it. The reward is a personal encounter with him, in which he confirms his love and acceptance in spite of our impoverished state. And it leads us to a life of service, to the privilege of being co-workers with him in the task of world evangelisation.

'My child, do you truly love me?'

'Oh, Father. You know all things. You know me better than I know myself. I can't deceive you, and I don't want to pretend to be something I'm not. But yes, I do love you, with all that I am I love you. I am yours, and I long to be able to serve you, just as I am. Thank you for accepting me, for loving me, for wanting me. Lord, put me in your kingdom wherever I can best serve you. And if you can be glorified through my life, use me. You know that I love you.'

10

First Hezekiah, Chapter 4

You should have seen their faces. Poor things, they didn't know what to think of me. They were all good, North American evangelicals, decent and orderly, educated from their youth in the line of thought of their denomination, and they were not used to being confronted with perspectives from other Christian traditions. They were making a 'missionary visit', getting to know the needs of the 'field', and that's how they came to be spending a few days with us. In one of the devotional meetings, in which I was going to be sharing with them, first of all each one was reading and commenting on one of their favourite verses of the Bible. It came to my turn.

'Wouldn't you like to give us one of your favourite verses before you speak to us?'

'OK,' I said, and started to read.

Blessed is God who lives for ever,
and blessed is his kingdom.
For he afflicts, and he shows mercy . . .
Acknowledge him before the nations, O sons of Israel;

for he has scattered us among them.

Make his greatness known there,

and exalt him in the presence of all the living;

because he is our Lord and God,

he is our Father for ever . . .

Praise the Lord of righteousness,

and exalt the King of the ages.

I give him thanks in the land of my captivity,

and I show his power and majesty to a nation of sinners . . .

O Jerusalem, the holy city . . .

Many nations will come from afar to the name of the Lord God,

bearing gifts in their hands, gifts for the King of heaven.

Generations of generations will give you joyful praise . . .

for they will be gathered together,

and will praise the Lord of the righteous.

'That's great, brother. Where were you reading from? Wasn't that Isaiah? Which chapter?'

'No, it wasn't Isaiah,' I replied. 'It was the book of Tobit, chapter 13, a selection from verses 1 to 12.'

Silence. Total silence. Some of those who still did not know their Bibles very well were looking for the book among the minor prophets; one was even looking in the index, and then peeping over at his neighbour to see if he had found it. But most of them just looked dumbfounded, as if I had read from the non-existent book of Hezekiah, or perhaps the Bhagavad Gita, or even (God help us!) the Catholic catechism. I had dared to quote from the Apocrypha.

May I just mention here that I am not in the habit of doing this! I am not quite sure what came over me that morning. I had just finished a period of extended prayer and fasting, and perhaps was wanting to let my hair down. I don't really know. But, overcome by a 'superfluity of naughtiness' (James 1:21 AV), I decided to read them these verses from an apocryphal work which had so caught my attention recently when studying about the life of Israel in the intertestamental period. Actually, I must do it again some time – it really was quite fun. . .

As I have already said, not everything in our Bibles is inspired by God – not everything in *my* Bible at least. You see, I am in the habit of using an edition of the Bible known as *Dios Habla Hoy* ('God Speaks Today', roughly equivalent to the Good News Bible) which contains the Apocrypha. This is not because I believe that these books are inspired or canonical, which I don't, or even 'deutero-canonical' (that is, from the 'second canon'), but simply because it gives me a Bible with the official seal of approval of the Catholic Church. In a country of nominal Catholics, amongst whom there are well-founded suspicions of the proliferation of sects, especially the Jehovah's Witnesses with their own 'version' of the Bible, it is very helpful to be able to show the comforting words of one of 'their' bishops in its opening pages.

A quick read of the books of the Apocrypha reveals that they are not inspired. They are not of the same 'quality' as the canonical books. But neither are they diabolical or 'dangerous', and until relatively recently they were always included in the Bible, despite not being part of the canon, being read by all kinds of believers. 'Apocryphal' does not mean 'heretical', 'false' or 'untrustworthy', as we often think it does today. It simply means 'hidden', in reference to the Jewish tradition contained in 4 Ezra 14:44–47:

So during the forty days ninety-four books were written. And when the forty days were ended, the Most High spoke to me, saying, 'Make public the twenty-four books that you wrote first and let the worthy and the unworthy read them; but keep the seventy that were written last, in order to give them to the wise among your people. For in them is the spring of understanding, the fountain of wisdom, and the river of knowledge.'

The 'first ones' mentioned here are the 24 books which make up the Hebrew Bible. (These 24 are the same as the 39 books of our Old Testament, but grouped together differently – see chapter 11 for more details.) The other 70 are made up of two groups. First, those genuine historical, wisdom and prophetic writings which fall outside the Jewish canon and which are known as the Apocrypha. Most of these are considered as canonical by the Catholic and/or Orthodox Churches. And secondly, the 'pseudepigrapha': books written by a third person using the name of a biblical author in an attempt to give their work more credibility – in other words, frauds, but pious ones! The dividing line between apocryphal and pseudepigraphal books is not totally clear. None of them can be considered as inspired, but they are useful for our Christian lives and are worthy of being read and studied.

Although there are no direct quotes, the New Testament contains more than 100 references and allusions to the apocryphal books, which demonstrates how familiar the apostolic authors were with their content. (Compare, for example, John 1:1–3 and Ecclesiasticus 24:3; Wisdom 7:21; 8:6; 9:1, 9; or Ephesians 6:11–17 with Wisdom 5:17–23; or Acts 26:6–8 with 2 Maccabees 7:9, 23, among many others.) This is only natural, as the apocryphal books are included in the Greek translation, the Septuagint, used by the apostles and the early church.

But there are direct quotes from other non-canonical authors. Jude quotes directly from one of the pseudepigraphal books in his epistle, which delayed its acceptance into the canon of Scripture. The story of Michael arguing with the devil over the body of Moses (v. 9) is taken from the 'Ascension of Moses', a Jewish text from the first century; and in verses 13–15 he quotes from the book of Enoch, an apocryphal text from the second century BC, which is currently considered canonical by the Ethiopian Church. In naming Jannes and Jambres as opponents of Moses in 2 Timothy 3:8, Paul is quoting from a Jewish *haggadah* (sacred text), and he makes reference to another *midrash* (didactical Jewish text) in 1 Corinthians 10:4. We can see that they read more than just the 24 'safe' books.

Most Protestants consider the Apocrypha to belong purely to the domain of the Catholic Church, but historically this is far from being the case. Whilst rejecting their canonicity, the early Reformers maintained their appreciation of the Apocrypha as useful for the Christian life, and these books were included in their Bibles, albeit in a separate section. This was the case with the first Protestant translation into Spanish, done by Casiodoro de la Reina and published in 1569, and in the later revision by Cipriano de Valera of 1602. In the 'Exhortation to the Reader' which serves as an introduction to his translation, Valera quotes contemporary scholars to defend the reading of the Apocrypha, but their exclusion from the canon. He does his utmost to demonstrate which are the canonical and which are the apocryphal books, thus participating in the debate sparked off by the Reformation and the inclusion of some of the apocryphal books in the Catholic Bible after the Council of Trent.

The King James version (AV), the 'standard' version for the English-speaking world during almost four centuries, also initially included the Apocrypha. And what's more, it was decreed that no edition of the Bible should be published without them. It was only at the beginning of the nineteenth century, when the International Bible Society began to distribute the Bible in earnest, that it became customary to print the Bible without them – a decision taken for purely economical, rather than theological, reasons. In the same way today we often print versions of the New Testament separately, and these are given away in evangelistic campaigns instead of whole Bibles. Why? Because we don't believe the Old Testament is important? Of course not – it is for financial reasons (although the neglect of the Old Testament and a growing lack of understanding of its message have been the secondary consequences of this process).

In spite of these historical roots, there are few evangelical believers these days who have read the apocryphal books, and those who have studied them are viewed with suspicion, not to mention anyone who dares to carry around a Bible which includes the Apocrypha. But we have any number of other writings, commentaries, concordances, even hymnals, attached to our Bibles, without anyone getting upset. And the Apocrypha, considered so important by our brothers throughout history, including even the New Testament writers themselves, are left behind and forgotten, or limited to those dubiously ecumenical brothers who come dangerously close to the ranks of the Catholic Church.

That's not how we ought to think of them. Even though they are not inspired, the apocryphal books form part of our Christian heritage and studying them is important for understanding our faith. They are useful for the building up of believers even if they are not sources of doctrine. Let's look at why.

In the Bible we find two periods of 400 years which are empty of prophetic activity and without biblical narrative: from the end of Genesis to the beginning of Exodus, and between the Old and New Testaments. Between Malachi and John the Baptist there is a gap of more than 450 years, in which God did not speak prophetically to his people. But 1,000 years before Malachi, the people of Israel had passed through a similar period in which they did not hear the voice of God, between Joseph and Moses. Four hundred years being fashioned in the protective womb of Egypt, until one day they were sufficiently developed for God to bring them forth as an independent nation.

However, we do know what happened during that time. Exodus 1 gives us a brief outline of their sufferings, the background we need to understand the account of Israel's deliverance from Pharaoh by the hand of Moses. Can you imagine how much you would understand if this chapter didn't exist, if we read straight from Genesis 50 to Exodus 2, without having the faintest idea what had happened in between? It would be a little confusing, to say the least.

The same thing happens with the period of silence between the Old and New Testaments. God has not left us with any canonical texts from this time, but has provided ample historical material which introduces us to the facts and events. And, even more important for the study of the

New Testament, it also reveals the development of Judaic thought and the formation of the world into which Jesus burst and in which the early church was built. Who were the Pharisees and Sadducees, for example? And why was Jesus' 'sin' against the temple and against the Law of Moses so important to them? Without knowing anything about intertestamental literature, it is impossible to understand these basic concepts and, in consequence, to understand the actions of our Lord.

Let's look at one concrete example. The people of Israel had always had 'the gospel' to be able to receive the blessing of God in their lives, and in turn to be a blessing to the nations (see Genesis 12:1–2; Galatians 3:8). However, we already know that as their history unfolded they became an ethnocentric people who denied the nations access to their God. They converted Yahweh into a tribal, regional God, bound like any common idol to the limits of a geographical area, instead of proclaiming him as Universal Creator, and Saviour of all those who call on his name, whatever their nationality or racial and cultural origin. They locked the God of all the peoples up in a Jewish temple and expected everyone else to convert to Judaism in order to be able to approach him.

But God does not let himself be locked up, and when we are incapable of understanding his commands, or if, having understood them, we refuse to obey, he opens another way. In 586 bc the 'sacred' temple was destroyed and the Jewish people, now reduced to an all-time low with a population of around 150,000, were carried off into captivity. What on earth was going on? Why had God allowed it? And now what? 'How can we sing the songs of the LORD while in a foreign land?' (Psalm 137:4). How can we worship God in a foreign country? The unthinkable had happened, and they had no idea how to live out their faith in the new circumstances in which they found themselves.

But it seems the penny finally dropped. Bit by bit they began to understand that they had been disobedient to God and that, since they had refused to bless the nations with his message of salvation, he had taken them there, to those very same pagan nations, so that, living subject to them, they might preach the glories of their God. While they had been so self-preoccupied with *their* temple, *their* king, *their* nation, the blessing of Abraham which God had promised *them*, they were blind to the real purpose of God: blessing the nations through them. But now they had no choice, and they began to give testimony to the only true God among the peoples of the earth.

This is why Tobit says:

> Acknowledge him before the nations, O sons of Israel;
> for he has scattered us among them.
> Make his greatness known there,
> and exalt him in the presence of all the living;
> because he is our Lord and God,
> he is our Father for ever . . .
> I give him thanks in the land of my captivity,
> and I show his power and majesty to a nation of sinners.
> (Tobit 13:3–4, 6)

Babylon, Persia, then Greece with its empire, and finally the Roman Empire, all had witness of the God of Israel and his message of salvation and blessing for all the peoples and all the nations. It is not that the Jews were great missionaries.

Far from it. But they stopped hiding their message about the almighty God within the limits of a temple service and allowed the nations to see the light shining in their midst. And the hand of God was with them. Whether it was due to a blessing of fertility and survival of their children, or whether it was the blessing of many converts who were added to the Jewish community during the exile, at the time of Jesus it is estimated that there were between six and eight million Jews in the Roman Empire, or to put it another way, 10 per cent of the total population, and 25 per cent of the population of the Middle East, were Jews.

This population growth is visible too in the pages of the New Testament. The Gospels show us a number of God-fearing Gentiles, for example the Roman centurion (Luke 7:1–10), or the Syro-Phoenician woman (Mark 7:24–30). The book of Acts tells of city after city where there were a good number of 'devout converts to Judaism' (13:43), 'God-fearing Greeks' (17:4), or 'God-fearing women' (13:50). Among them, for example, we find Lydia, 'a worshipper of God' (16:14), and Justus, also 'a worshipper of God' (18:7). In all of these phrases the Greek word being translated is *sebomai*, 'to worship', which was used especially for those proselytes who had become convinced of the truth of the God of Israel but who did not want to fulfil the whole Law and become Jews, generally rejecting the practice of circumcision. But they were worshippers of God, they feared him, and they met together with those who had accepted this rite and become 100 per cent Jews.

It is not strange, therefore, that these people accepted the gospel once it was preached to them. They already knew that Yahweh was their God, that salvation was found in him. But now they were being offered the chance to approach him and be completely accepted without undergoing any foreign rites or losing their national and cultural identity. God had prepared the ground. In those 500 years, more or less, the Jewish faith had ceased to be the insignificant tribal religion of an obstinate people group in Palestine, and had developed into the only 'universal' faith which knew neither political nor ethnic boundaries. In Jesus the door was opened wide to the Gentiles. However, it was a door founded upon the workings of God through his people during the intertestamental period.

I really ought to finish this chapter here. We have examined the importance of the apocryphal books for our faith today, and I don't want to waste words. But I cannot finish without making a brief comparison between the situation of Israel during this period, the early church, and our churches today.

Perhaps, we think, this sin of omission in the Jewish people is forgivable. After all, many of our scholars today don't see the missionary message of the Old Testament either, so it's hardly very surprising that the Jews themselves didn't understand it and turned their universal religion into an exclusive club. Perhaps – although the Old Testament communicates the responsibility of God's people to be a blessing to the nations clearly enough, for those who want to hear its message.

But the early church? That's a different kettle of fish. They (like the churches of our day) had received a clear, specific mission mandate, called the 'Great Commission'. Jesus had promised them power to take the gospel to the ends of the earth. And what did they do? Well, they got together, planned their strategy, engaged in spiritual warfare, and . . . stayed in Jerusalem! It seems they suffered from 'base fever', a scourge for which no vaccine has been found even up to the present day. In spite of all they had received straight from the mouth of their Lord, they remained captive to their ethnocentricity and lack of understanding of the purposes of God, and committed the 'Great Omission'.

Nevertheless, God is not limited by the vicissitudes of his people; he is not caught by surprise. If his people are not able to obey Acts 1:8, well, he sends them an Acts 8:1: 'On that day a great persecution broke out against the church at Jerusalem, and all except the apostles were scattered throughout Judea and Samaria . . . Those who had been scattered preached the word wherever they went' (Acts 8:1, 4). It's that simple. As the English poet Steve Turner said, 'History repeats herself. Has to. No one listens.' Once again the people of God found themselves victims of an unjust persecution which took the believers to the places where *God* wanted them to be – among the nations. And once again God was glorified among the peoples of the world, despite the slowness of his people.

And today, are we any different? Haven't we received the same clear mandate from our Lord? Don't we have at our disposal impressive resources for carrying out the task which he has given us? Has he not blessed us more than at any other time in human history? Why, then, is it so difficult for us to bow down to his authority and attend to his command to preach the gospel to the nations? Why are we so preoccupied with our buildings, which get bigger and bigger and more and more ornate, when 'David's fallen tent', the testimony among the nations (Acts 15:16), is still in ruins? How long will we continue to ignore the avalanches of refugees and immigrants from 'closed' Islamic countries inundating the countries of Europe from precisely those countries where we have not taken the gospel? Is it possible that God is trying to tell us something here? It is time we learned from history. God has blessed us, and so richly. But he has blessed us so that we can be a channel of blessing for all the families of the earth. Let's recapture what is important for him, as the people did in the time of Tobit. Let's not lose sight of *his* priorities in enjoying all that he has given us – it could cost us very dearly.

11

And Did You Also Know. . .

. . .that the order of the books in our Bibles, at least in the Old Testament, is not inspired?

Sometimes I hear all kinds of comments about the purpose of God in placing the books of the Bible in the order in which we find them in our Bibles: that they ought to be read in this order; that if God had wanted us to read Isaiah before Leviticus (which I would recommend to any new believer who is about to read the Old Testament for the first time), he would have put it first; and any number of similar statements. Maybe they're right, I don't know, but it doesn't fit in with the facts.

This matter of the order of the books in our Bibles is a relatively recent phenomenon. It certainly didn't worry anyone in Jesus' day. From the times of Moses up to Jesus the writings of the Old Testament were kept on *scrolls*, not on pages fixed into books. These rolls were stored in a special cupboard in the synagogue, and taken out as they were needed. They were all piled up in there, without thought as to which was on top or underneath – they all contained the Word of God. Even today in a Jewish synagogue the Torah is read from scrolls, not books.

It was only with the use of parchment instead of papyrus for writing, and the later invention of the 'codex', a type of book made up of various sheets of parchment inside two thin pieces of wood, that it became necessary to think about the order of the books of the Bible. The codex format rapidly gained supremacy among believers as the best format for transmitting and preserving their Scriptures. And thus the order of the books became standardised.

But how was the order decided? In the case of the New Testament there was no established precedent, and we cannot comment on those decisions. The same church which during successive Councils decided the canon of the New Testament also defined the order in which those books were added to the Hebrew Scriptures. And the Old Testament?

You would have expected that the order which had been finally settled on for the Hebrew Bible would be followed, but that was not in fact the case. The contents of the Hebrew Bible – that is, the identification of the canonical books as well as their order – took shape, under God's guidance, over centuries as God's people discerned the prophetic voice beyond the Torah of Moses. The first declaration on the extent of the Hebrew canon as such, probably itself made to counter growing Christian use of the Scriptures, came around the end of the first century at the Council of Jamnia, being confirmed and preserved in the work of the Masorete scribes 800 years later. And, to our surprise, it is completely different. To start with, they consider that there are only 24 books where we have 39, grouping the minor prophets as one, likewise the books of 1 and 2 Samuel, 1 and 2 Kings, and 1 and 2 Chronicles, and treating Ezra and Nehemiah as a single book. It starts with the Pentateuch, followed by the historical books of Joshua up to 2 Kings, minus Ruth, then the prophets, starting with the major ones (minus Daniel), and then the minor ones, continuing with Psalms and Proverbs, Job, Song of Songs, Ruth, Lamentations, Ecclesiastes, Esther, Daniel, Ezra, Nehemiah and 1 and 2 Chronicles. Their Bible does not end with the words of Malachi, therefore, but with the decree of Cyrus inviting the people of God to return to Jerusalem.

So where did the order of the books in our Bibles come from? It came from the version known as the Septuagint, often abbreviated as LXX, which, according to the tradition contained in the apocryphal letter of Aristeas, was completed by a group of 70 scholarly Hebrews sent to Alexandria at the request of the librarian of that famous city in the third century BC. Although there may not be much truth in that tale, the Septuagint translation was certainly started around that time, and was in circulation well before Jamnia. It was produced at the demand of the Jews themselves for a translation into Greek, since the majority of those living in the Diaspora had lost the use of Aramaic, didn't know any Hebrew at all, and needed the Scriptures in their native tongue, Greek. Indeed, the events which brought the LXX into being would seem to be part of the whole process by which the Old Testament canon itself was decided. Its text provides an early witness to the most likely meaning of obscure Hebrew texts and is regularly used by modern translators in such cases.

It was this translation which came to be the 'believers' Bible', being adopted by the early Christians for their devotional reading and for their evangelistic efforts. It became the bastion of the Christian faith, the cornerstone of its very existence and the tool for its multiplication. Perhaps it was natural for them to follow the order of this translation when making the first Bibles, comprised of the text of the Septuagint Old Testament and the books of the New Testament, all in Greek. The curious thing is that this order was maintained even in the first masterly translation into Latin, known as the 'Vulgate', which was to become the Bible of Roman Catholicism, taking precedence over even the Greek and Hebrew originals. (Incidentally, 'Vulgate' simply refers to the 'vulgar' language, as the people spoke it. There was nothing holy, religious or special about it – it was the language of the people, and the 'Latin' church would have done well to follow this principle of putting the Word of God in the language of the people throughout its long and turbulent history.) Its translator, Hieronimus, worked from the Hebrew text, but such was the established tradition that he did not adopt the Hebrew order of books, but rather left them as they are found in the Septuagint.

The Septuagint must be one of the most neglected areas of Christian investigation, yet it is one of the most important for a correct understanding of New Testament Greek, whose vocabulary and grammar it follows in an extraordinary way. It is incredible how a simple translation has held greater influence than the original itself in something as basic as the order of books in the Old Testament – a fact of which few are aware. But it has exercised an even greater influence in the creation of the New Testament, and in a way that has transcendental importance for the work of missions. We shall look at this in the next chapter.

12

Do You Understand What You Are Reading?

'*Allahu Akbar. Allahu Akbar.*' 'God is Great. God is Great.' Within range of the call to prayer sounding insistently from the nearby minaret, I sat down on the ground to talk to the young lad who was reading the Koran. It was open at the most famous *Surah*, or chapter, of the holy book of Islam, and he was reciting with evident pride: '*Bismillah arrahman arrahim, alham-dulilah, arrabi alalamin.*' To his great surprise, I repeated the words with him, and a cheerful smile lit up his face. A *kafir*, an infidel, could read and recite his Koran.

After I had listened to him recite for a while, we began to talk in French and I asked him, like the evangelist of old, 'Do you understand what you're reading?'

'Not a word!' he answered me, surprised by the question. 'They have to explain it to me, but the important thing is to be able to say it properly, not to understand what it means.' And with that he went back to his reading, the blind recitation of a text in a language that was foreign to him, imagining that in this way he was pleasing God, and even getting to know him more.

Today we so much take for granted the availability of a translation of the Bible in our own language. And we don't only have one, but lots, from which we can choose the one that suits us. We no longer live in the days when the mass was only said in Latin, and it was a capital sin to read the Bible in your own language. Many people paid with their lives so that the Bible could be translated into vernacular languages and distributed to those who wanted to read it, so that we could have the freedom we enjoy today to meet and read together.

Islam is not like that. The Koran is 'untranslatable', being written in the 'language of heaven'. You will never find a 'translation' of the Koran; they are called 'commentaries' or 'interpretations'. One version, for example, is entitled 'The Meaning of the Glorious Koran', but it is not considered a translation. The Koran should not and cannot be translated, basically because the Islamic concept of inspiration or revelation does not permit it. It is quite different from the Christian concept.

According to Islam, Mohammed was not 'inspired'. Rather, he received a 'recitation' from the angel Gabriel, who was reading from the 'mother-book' which exists in heaven, in Arabic of course. Neither human, temporal nor socio-cultural factors entered into it – the Koran is an earthly copy of the heavenly original that exists eternally with God. How could its contents ever be expressed in merely human languages? (Indeed, this is one of the weakest points of Islamic theology, the existence of an eternal and unchanging 'Word of God' which is with Allah, as it comes dangerously close to the greatest sin according to Islam, *shirq* or blasphemy, making someone or something equal with God.)

(Here we open another parenthesis. What's all this about a heavenly language? Wouldn't it be rather strange if God spoke in the Arabic dialect of Mohammed, a Semitic language from the Arabian Peninsula in the seventh century? Or any other human language, including Hebrew, limited in space and time to a restricted group of speakers? In fact, 'Hebrew' as one entity does not actually exist, and the Bible itself shows the constant development of the language, the later texts using a very different 'Hebrew' from the earlier ones. Which one does God speak? How is it possible that God has always spoken the same language, if in reality that language itself is the product of centuries of linguistic evolution?

Many experiments have been done to 'prove' that God speaks this or that language, from Hebrew [of course] and Arabic, on to English, German and Chinese. In the thirteenth century it is said that the Holy Roman Emperor Frederick II of Hohenstaufen copied the methodology used by Pharaoh Psametic of Egypt 2,000 years earlier, in having two infants brought up by a deaf-mute servant, supposing that in this way the true language of heaven would be revealed. They learned to 'communicate' using a few grunts and died before pronouncing a single word. The same fate was suffered later by children brought up by a Turkish governor trying to demonstrate that Arabic was the language of heaven.

In the Bible, whenever God speaks, he uses the language of the one he is speaking to. Whether we think of the Spirit who spoke to Ananias, or the word of God which first came to Abram, he did not need to teach them a celestial language first; he spoke to them in their native tongue. And what about 'angelic' languages? In the same way, when we hear an angel speak through the pages of the Bible, be it in dream, vision or actually present, he speaks the language of the person who receives the message. As we can see, either they have great linguistic capacities, or perhaps communication in heaven is more a thing of the heart and doesn't need to pass through brain, mouth and ears as in our case. But anyway, let's get back to our theme.)

It's not just the Koran which is untranslatable; the whole practice of Islamic religion is trapped in the concepts and practices of the seventh century. Style of dress, laws, interpersonal relationships across the whole of society, everything is submitted to the lifestyle and aspirations of an Arab merchant of that era. As they see it, God revealed his eternal and untranslatable word through this medium, and the ideal human society was frozen from that moment on.

Thank God that our concept of revelation does not lead us to these conclusions, but permits us to contextualise the eternal message of the gospel in our temporal reality, including the translation of God's Word. We believe that God *inspired* the biblical authors, but each one wrote in his own human language, recording his own unique style in his writings as well. Although the exact same language is used, the way Mark writes Greek is not the same as that of John, nor is Isaiah's usage of Hebrew the same as that of Jeremiah. They used a normal and everyday human language, impregnated not only with the socio-cultural customs of their time, but with their own personality too.

Thanks to this 'humanity' in the languages of the Bible, we also understand that God has authorised the process of translation of his message into every human language. There are no 'sacred' languages that are better suited to religious expression than others. Latin is not the 'holy vehicle' for the biblical message; it was the vernacular of the Roman people in the third century AD, and nothing more. Even the dialect of Greek contained in the New Testament itself is not classical Greek, the Attic variety used by the famous Hellenic writers. Apart from the first four verses of Luke – where it seems the author is establishing his credentials as a learned historian before getting on with the real job of communicating with his potential readers – the New Testament is written in the everyday language of the people, *koiné* Greek, or 'common' Greek (from where we get the word *koinonia*, or 'communion'). God wants his Word expressed in the languages of people's hearts.

The first serious translation that was made of the Old Testament, as we saw, was the Greek version called the Septuagint, or LXX. It was the product of the efforts of various people during the three centuries before Christ, and made the Word of God accessible to the Jewish people of the Diaspora in what had become the native language of most. But was the translation inspired by God? Or was it the product of human wisdom, fallible and imperfect?

The legend contained in the apocryphal letter of Aristeas claims that it was the result of divine inspiration – that 70 scholars, working independently, arrived at the same translation. But a superficial examination shows us that it is a human translation, even very human in places. There are parts that do not follow the Hebrew very well, that paraphrase it in an unacceptable way, but others follow the Hebrew very rigidly, transferring into the Greek a variety of 'Hebrewisms', and even the grammatical structure of the Hebrew itself.

As an aside, it is not only the Septuagint that does this – it happens in our modern translations as well. Archaic or wooden word-for-word structure is to be expected in older translations, where we find some real beauties. I honestly doubt that any of the following, taken from the AV, are at all clear to the majority of modern readers. When Saul went into the cave to 'cover his feet' (1 Samuel 24:3), would you realise that he was actually going to the toilet? How many of us would automatically know that a 'molten sea' (1 Kings 7:23) is in fact a die-cast basin; that 'fell on his neck' (Luke 15:20) does not mean 'tripped over'; or that 'shutteth up his bowels' (1 John 3:17) has nothing to do with Saul's activity just mentioned, but rather means 'to refuse to have com-passion, to close one's heart'? And as for 'gird up the loins of your mind' (1 Peter 1:13), it is perhaps possible to guess what this means, but it is not at all obvious, and depends on the ingenuity of the reader, not on the clarity of the trans-lation's communication. Unfortunately, such obstacles to proper understanding of God's Word are not entirely absent from newer translations either. Psalm 1:1 in the NIV criticises those who 'stand in the way of sinners', using a phrase whose natural meaning would be 'to oppose sinners', something the text is not talking about at all. The GNB's 'fol-low the example of sinners' is much clearer. And what on earth does the NIV's 'Look at them putting the branch to their nose!' of Ezekiel 8:17 mean? Anyway, let's get back to the Septuagint.

At times, it has to be said, the Septuagint is not a 'good' translation, and any 'revision committee' would have made quite a few alterations to a second edition. It certainly cannot claim to be the result of 'inspiration from God'. Like any other translation of the Bible today, it is the work of fallible human hands, arguable in some aspects and with room for improvement. Even though God may have helped the translators in their work, it is not inspired by God.

Well, so what? We have established that the Septuagint version is not inspired by God, but that's just a translation; it's not in the Bible, so what's all the fuss about? What does it have to do with our subject?

Let's answer that question with another question. Have you ever noticed that when the New Testament authors quote from the Old Testament, sometimes the quotation does not exactly follow the original reading? That in some cases it is quite different, and completely changes the meaning? In Matthew 21, for example, during the triumphal entrance into Jerusalem, Jesus quotes from Psalm 8 and says, 'From the lips of children and infants you have ordained praise' (Matthew 21:16). However, if we look at the original verse in Psalm 8:2, we find that it says, 'From the lips of children and infants you have ordained *strength.*' (See NIV footnote: the Hebrew term *oz*, used 93 times in the Old Testament, is consistently translated as 'strength' in the NIV – see Psalm 21:1, 13; 28:7–8, for example – but is rendered 'praise' here to harmonise with the quote in Matthew. While understandable, this is not acceptable practice in a version that purports to be a translation and not an interpretation.)

Here is another example, quoting again from this psalm.

Let's read Hebrews 2:7. Referring to humanity, it says, 'You made him a little lower than the angels.' It is a quotation from Psalm 8:5, which says, 'You made him a little lower than the heavenly beings.' (The Hebrew term used here is *elohim*, which is translated as 'heavenly beings' rather than 'God', although this is given as an alternative in a footnote in the NIV. This is the only time in the 2,606 occasions where this word is used when it is translated thus, and the translators appear to have again allowed themselves to be influenced by the New Testament quotation; *elohim* is the plural form in Hebrew, but it is normally used to refer to God as an 'emphatic plural'. It can also mean 'the gods', but on no other occasion does it refer to angels.) The Hebrew puts 'lower than God', but quoting this in the New Testament, the author of the epistle to the Hebrews puts 'angels'. Lower than God or lower than the angels? Quite a difference.

Another psalm. In Hebrews 10:5 the author quotes from Psalm 40:6, and tells us, 'Sacrifice and offering you did not desire, but a body you prepared for me.' Let's look at the original Hebrew: 'Sacrifice and offering you did not desire, but my ears you have pierced.' Again, in Revelation 2:27, speaking of the nations of the world, we read, 'He will rule them with an iron sceptre,' quoting from Psalm 2:8. This, however, reads, 'You will break them with a rod of iron' (see NIV footnote).

And it's not just in quotes from the Psalms that we find these differences. In 1 Peter 5:5 the apostle quotes from Proverbs 3:34 thus: 'God opposes the proud but gives grace to the humble.' In the original Hebrew we read, 'He mocks proud mockers but gives grace to the humble.' The strange thing is that James quotes this verse exactly the same as

Peter, not following the original Hebrew reading either (James 4:6).

Isaiah is also quoted in this rather odd way. In Matthew 12:21, the former publican tells us, 'In his name the nations will put their hope,' while in Isaiah 42:4 we read, 'In his law the islands will put their hope.' And Peter quotes from Isaiah 28:16 thus: 'See, I lay a stone in Zion, a chosen and precious cornerstone, and the one who trusts in him will never be put to shame' (1 Peter 2:6). But in the original we find: 'See, I lay a stone in Zion, a tested stone, a precious cornerstone for a sure foundation; the one who trusts will never be dismayed.'

And how many people accompanied Jacob to Egypt? Was it 75 (Acts 7:14)? Or was it 70 (Genesis 46:27)? Did Jacob lean on the top of his staff (Hebrews 11:21) or bow down at the head of his bed (Genesis 47:31, NIV footnote)? And was it a virgin who was going to be with child (Matthew 1:23) or a young woman (Isaiah 7:14)? (The Hebrew word *almah* used in this verse from Isaiah should not be translated as 'virgin', since it refers to a young woman who may or may not be married. Most of our translations have allowed themselves to be influenced by Christian thinking on the virgin birth of Christ, but this idea is not actually contained in the Hebrew. It *is* found, however, in the Greek text of Matthew, where the word *parthenos* is used, which refers exclusively to a person who has not had sexual relations.)

Let's look at one final example. In Hebrews 1:6 the author quotes from Deuteronomy 32:43 thus: 'Let all God's angels worship him,' while the quotation in the Hebrew Old Testament actually reads, 'Rejoice, O nations, with his people.' And a curious observation – this verse is quoted 'correctly' by Paul in Romans 15:10. There, the apostle makes a literal translation from the Hebrew into the Greek in which he is writing, and so it appears totally distinct from the quotation in the book of Hebrews, although both are actually citing the same Old Testament reference.

I think we have seen enough, although we could carry on for several more pages. What is happening here? Why so much discrepancy in these passages from the Old Testament quoted in the New? The reason is actually quite simple. When they wanted to quote their scriptures, the apostolic authors did not usually look up the corresponding scroll from the Torah or the prophets, find the quotation, and translate it literally into Greek as they wrote. They usually did one of two things. Either they quoted from memory, giving rise to all kinds of variations in the end result (as happens with us when we do this, quoting from the 'version according to my humble self'). Or, much more often, they went to their Bible – the Greek Septuagint – and quoted from this translation, just as we do. There are very few of us who look up the meaning of the original and make our own translation when we want to quote something. We simply quote from the Bible we normally use, and that's what they did too.

Seventy-five per cent of the Old Testament quotations in the New Testament are taken from the Septuagint, and are not literal translations from the Hebrew Scriptures. Normally the authors copied directly from this version instead of making the effort to do their own translation from the Hebrew, as is perfectly understandable. As we saw in the case of Paul in Romans 15:10, sometimes they did, but it wasn't the norm.

Now most of the time you can hardly tell, since the Greek
of the Septuagint is generally quite similar to the Hebrew
text, and the difference might only be perceived in one particular word, in the exact tense of a verb, or in the word
order. But on other occasions there is a marked difference,
as in the texts quoted above. In each of these the difference
can be attributed to this practice: all were quoted from the
Greek Septuagint version, and not from the Hebrew. We
looked at Matthew 1:23, for example, quoting from Isaiah
7:14, where the Septuagint does translate the Hebrew as
parthenos. This is not an exact translation, since it limits the
identity of the young woman to a young virgin. Interest-
ingly, this effectively establishes that the concept of the virgin birth was not an unfamiliar idea to the pre-Christian
Jews who were responsible for the Septuagint translation,
nor was it a propagandist invention of the first Christians.
As early Christians took hold of the Septuagint and used it
for their own evangelistic purposes – including reference to
this verse – it was summarily dropped by the Jews in favour
of alternative translations which rapidly arose, such as
those of Aquila and Theodotion from the second century.
Although apparently comfortable in Hebrew, and addressing his Gospel primarily to the Jews, Matthew quoted
directly from the Septuagint as this best expressed the
prophetic reality of what had happened at Jesus' birth.

We are looking at a phenomenon of which the majority
of people are unaware, but which has significance of truly
enormous proportions, if we are prepared to hear what God
wants to say to us through it. 'He who has ears, let him
hear.'

The texts of the Old Testament are inspired by God. Those

of the New Testament also. But the Greek translation of the Old Testament, the Septuagint, is not. However, those inspired texts of the New Testament include quotations not from the inspired Hebrew, but from a human translation, sometimes a bad or even incorrect one, within its inspired pages. What a mystery! That which is merely human is clothed with divinity and somehow elevated to the level of the Word of God. As he inspired the New Testament writers, God allowed them to include the fruit of imperfect human endeavour in what was to become his infallible Word to all humanity.

In this way God seems to be 'authorising' the process of the translation of his Word. He is putting his seal of approval on missionary effort. Even though it is not perfect, he wants this testimony of who he is to reach all the nations of the world in their own language. He is not a prisoner of the limitations of a human tongue, and is perfectly capable of communicating his Word through the vehicle of a defective translation. The law kills, but the Spirit gives life, and at the end of the day it seems that it does not matter whether the translation communicates the *exact* meaning or not. Of course, translators should take great pains to understand the meaning of the original and render it in the best way possible in the receiving language. But God's Spirit speaks through his Word, even in a translation which leaves much to be desired.

This singular use of the Septuagint in the New Testament reveals something more to us of the missionary heart of God, and his desire to make himself known among the nations. The important thing is that everyone should have access to the Word of God in a language they can understand, preferably in their native tongue. The church of Christ cannot rest until everyone has this opportunity. Fulfilling the Great Commission requires effort dedicated to the learning of languages and the translation of the Word of God. It is our responsibility to train and send workers who are capable and qualified to complete this task, if we really want the gospel to be preached to every nation.

Of course it matters which translation we use, and we should try to make sure that it follows the meaning of the originals as accurately as possible. It is good to compare translations, and learn something of the original languages. But we should not use all our energy arguing the validity of the dozens of translations available to us when the fact is that God speaks through each and every one of them – and when the majority of the world's population still cannot read the Bible in their mother tongue.

God is not a 'pernickety' God. He is a God who wants to talk, to communicate with humanity. If in ancient times he spoke through a donkey, can he not speak today through our imperfect efforts to take his Word to other nations? Although I may find it hard to learn another language, and I may never master it to perfection, isn't God able to use me as an instrument to reveal himself to another people? Can he not make his Word known, in spite of my human imperfections? Of course he can. Let's renew our commitment to him and to his Word, until everyone has heard it – in their own language.

13

Are We in Concordance?

Frank had one goal in life above all others, and now, close to death in his hospital bed, he could say that he had achieved it – or almost. He was ready to go to be with the Lord, and there were moments in his illness when he seemed to be more in the next life than in this one. He made Paul's words his own, 'I desire to depart and be with Christ, which is better by far' (Philippians 1:23). He even got angry with us for praying for him and asking the Lord to leave him with us for a little while longer.

And his goal? To be able to find any verse in the Bible without a concordance. He wanted to be able to give the chapter for any given text, however obscure and unknown it might be, and even the exact verse reference for most of them too. How we used to test him! Where, for example, do you find, 'The Lord has sent out his word against Jacob, and it has fallen upon Israel'? Or, 'If he wounds him with an instrument of iron and he dies, he has committed homicide: he who commits homicide shall die'? Not to mention 'Mica, Rehob, Hashabiah', or 'Ahiah, Hanan, Anan'?

He was a machine. He hardly ever made a mistake. We

used to call him 'the speaking concordance', and he inspired us all to try and get to know the Word of God better. When he finally died we gave thanks to God for his life and his example, and we had to start using our 'silent' concordances.

The concordance. Let's consider that section which we find at the end of our Bibles, or a good many of them. A useful tool for finding a verse in the Bible quickly, or for studying a specific theme when preparing a biblical message.

Obviously, this part of our Bibles was not inspired by God either. No concordance contained within a Bible is complete, since there is a limit to the number of pages and the size of even the weightiest study Bible. A concordance in a Bible will always reflect what the editor considers to be essential, and important references can be missing. To do a balanced study we cannot rely only on this. If we want a complete concordance, we will need to buy a separate volume.

But there is another way in which the sense of the biblical message can be lost. The concordances which we have in our Bibles are based, naturally, on the text of that particular translation. As such, they are not a concordance of the biblical texts and ideas in themselves, but of a translation of these. And that is not the same thing.

We have already seen that the sphere of reference of two languages is never exactly the same. One word in Hebrew, for example, can be translated into a great variety of words in English. And one single English word can represent many different words in the original. No concordance based on a translation will be able to reflect these subtleties.

A concordance is, in the end, nothing more than an 'index of uses' of any word. It shows us the full meaning of a term by relating it to its context. I live and work in Spain. It may well be that you don't speak a word of Spanish, and if I were to ask you the meaning of the word *mesa*, you would have no idea. But if I tell you that I have to set the *mesa* before I can sit down at the *mesa* to eat, and that I bought this *mesa* together with four chairs at the local MFI furniture warehouse, or its Spanish equivalent, you would have more of an idea. You wouldn't have to resort to a dictionary to know what it was – the context itself shows you.

This is how it works when we use a concordance of the original language. We begin to get more of an understanding of biblical words, not from a dictionary, nor from a translation (which never has exactly the same meaning), but from their use within the language of the Bible. Using a concordance of an English version teaches us more about the style of the translator than about the biblical word itself. The only way to open this treasure chest of biblical study is by using a Greek or Hebrew concordance.

It is impossible to follow the richness of the original thought without using a concordance of the original language. But don't panic, they are not difficult to use, and most of them can be handled easily even if we haven't the slightest knowledge of the biblical languages. If we can get hold of one which uses Strong's system of numbering biblical words, a universal system which assigns a particular number to every word used in the Greek and Hebrew texts of the Bible, it becomes even easier. (This system is used in most Bible computer programs and makes this type of study much simpler, without having to learn even the Greek or

Hebrew alphabet.) Interlinear Bibles are available which include these numbers along with the Greek and Hebrew in parallel lines.

Why is it so important? Isn't it enough just to read and study our Bibles? Do we all have to learn Greek and Hebrew? Of course not, that's not what it's about. We can get to know God and his Word perfectly well using our Bibles; they are respectable translations and have been produced with much care. However, other facets of the contents of the Bible can only be revealed to us by using this type of tool. It allows us to get closer to the original texts, even without learning the languages in which they were written. It can show us the continuity of thought of the author, the full meaning of biblical concepts that do not have a direct equivalent in English, and sometimes throws much light on the meaning of a word by comparing it with other uses of that word in the original, or with derivatives of it.

Let's look at the simple word 'separate' (*apartar*), for example. (Unless stated otherwise, the word studies used in this and the next paragraph refer to the corresponding Spanish words, given in italics, as used in the Reina-Valera 1960 translation. The principle, however, applies in like manner to any particular Bible translation.) Our concordance will tell us that this word is used 70 times in the New Testament. But what this tool for study does not tell us is that 'separate' is used to translate 30 different Greek words, each one with its own particular facet of meaning. The most common word is used only 10 times. Looking up this word in an English concordance doesn't really tell us much about the Bible itself.

The same thing occurs with other common words in the

New Testament. 'To pass' (*pasar*), which is found 124 times
in the Reina-Valera translation, takes the place of 39 words
in the original, and 'to take' (*llevar*), a verb used 134 times,
is the translation of 35 different Greek words. 'To cast'
(*echar*) is used to translate 43 different Greek words, 'to
come' (*venir*) 44, 'to receive' (*recibir*) 36, 'to take' (*tomar*) 38,
and, leaving the best till last, 'to put' (*poner*) translates 54
different Greek verbs. What does it teach us when we look
up one of these words, or many others like them, in a normal concordance? It may help us to find an unknown reference for a text, but it teaches us nothing about the true
use of the word in the Bible.

So far we have looked at the case of one single word in
English being used to translate a large number of words in
the original language. The same thing happens the other
way round, when a Greek or Hebrew word is translated
into various different words in English.

Let's take the word 'fellowship' (*comunión*), for example.
It is found 10 times in the Reina-Valera New Testament.
This time it always translates the same Greek word,
koinonia. So that's quite simple, then, isn't it? Well, no. In
looking up 'fellowship' in our concordance, we would only
have found half of the occurrences of *koinonia* in the Scriptures. This is because *koinonia* has a much wider meaning
than that of simple 'fellowship', and four other translations
are found in the AV: 'communication', 'communion', 'contribution' and 'distribution'. ('Fellowship' is found 15 times
in the AV, translating three distinct Greek words.) It is
impossible to discover the full sense of biblical 'fellowship'
if we are not aware of these other uses of *koinonia* in the
New Testament.

Or we can consider another word, *dokimazo*, which is found in Romans 12:2, being translated there as 'prove' (AV). This word is used 22 times in the Greek New Testament, and is given seven different renderings in the English of the AV: 'allow', 'approve', 'discern', 'examine', 'like', 'prove', 'try'.

Let us look at one final example from the New Testament: *logos*, or 'word'. Whilst this is the most common translation, it is not the only one. In the AV we also find 'account', 'cause', 'communication', 'concerning', 'doctrine', 'fame', 'have to do', 'intent', 'matter', 'mouth', 'preaching', 'question', 'reason', 'reckon', 'rumour', 'saying', 'show', 'speaker', 'speech', 'talk', 'thing', 'tidings', 'treatise', 'utterance' and 'work' – in sum, 26 different English words for one in Greek.

The same picture is repeated in the Old Testament – one Hebrew word is translated into English using different words, and one English word is used to represent different terms from the original Hebrew. For example, *nefesh*, a word which is normally translated as 'soul', is also expressed in the AV as 'appetite', 'beast', 'body', 'breath', 'creature', 'dead', 'dead body', 'fish', 'ghost', 'heart', 'hearty', 'life', 'living creature', 'lust', 'man', 'mind', 'mortally', 'person', 'pleasure', 'self', 'senses', 'thing' and 'will'; that is, 23 words in addition to 'soul'. This is getting to be too much for a simple soul, one might be tempted to say.

However, we should not consider this as something that just complicates our study, but rather understand that it opens up new horizons for us in interpreting the Bible, and greater possibilities for receiving light and revelation from its pages. This type of study offers us the chance to perceive apparently insignificant details, which will contribute much to our understanding of God and his will.

This is the case with Isaiah 49:6. But before we delve into the exegesis of this latest example, let's try and place ourselves in the context of the verse.

The year is 701 BC. The forces of Assyria have just conquered the people of Israel, all the northern tribes have been taken captive, and will go on to disappear and be forgotten. Sennacherib is at the gates of Jerusalem threatening to do the same to the nation of Judah. However, their king Hezekiah cries out to God on behalf of the people, and God delivers them in an undeniably miraculous way. Praise be to Jah! (And by the way, if just one angel killed 185,000 of the army of Sennacherib [2 Kings 19:35], how much more would the 12 legions of angels, which the Father would have given to Jesus had he asked for them, been able to do [Matthew 26:53]? Let's go mad and do some crazy calculations: one legion consists of 6,000 men, so 12 legions would be 72,000. If these were angels, and each one were capable of killing 185,000 in one single night, Jesus had at his disposition the potential angelic power to destroy 13,320,000,000 people instantly – more than twice the current population of the planet, and 60 times the population in Jesus' day. It truly was not the nails that held our Lord on the cross; it was his unending love for you and me. But let's get back to 701 BC.)

What a wonderful miracle. But there is a prophet who knows that it will not always be like this. God has delivered this time, but he will not overlook the sin of his people for ever, and the day is drawing near when Judah will also be carried into captivity. It would not be by the hand of the Assyrians, but rather the Babylonians, and the people would not be destroyed, but would have to re-establish their identity with no homeland or structure of their own.

Writing more than 100 years before this event, Isaiah addresses the descendants of his people in captivity. Sometimes known as Deutero-Isaiah, chapters 40–66 of Isaiah deal prophetically with this stage in the life of Israel, and formed the complement to the 'direct' prophecy and teaching of Jeremiah and Ezekiel, who were both living and ministering at the start of the period of captivity. What should the attitude of the people of Israel be in that place? How should they live? What goals should they adopt? What would it mean to be a worshipper of Yahweh in exile?

For most of the Israelites it was pretty clear: Israel had to be restored as a nation; the temple had to be rebuilt; and Israel had to become the 'king of all the nations' once again. Their priority must be to wait for the opportunity to return to Zion and regather the people, who had been dispersed throughout the Babylonian and Persian kingdoms, around the new temple in Jerusalem. Any other option was unthinkable – they knew no other reality than the worship of Yahweh in *his* temple, built in *his* land, officiated by *his* priests, and under the protection of *his* chosen king.

However, as we have seen, bit by bit they began to realise that God had other plans for them. When finally, in 538 BC, the Persian king Cyrus decreed that they were free to return to Palestine and consigned to them an impressive logistical support, it was a sad little group that went back. The list of around 50,000 people recorded in Ezra 2 looks, at first glance, impressive, but it did not even make up 20 per cent of the total Israelite population, even less if we discount the foreign wives some of them had taken. Having understood that God wanted them among the nations, the rest stayed in Susa, Egypt and Babylon.

The prophecies of Isaiah were key in the development of this understanding, and among those we find Isaiah 49. It speaks about the 'Servant of the LORD', a figure who appears several times throughout these chapters of Isaiah and is difficult to identify. To whom does it refer? Sometimes to the whole nation of Israel, at other times to the promised messianic figure, and occasionally, as in this chapter, to the 'faithful remnant' of the people of God, the 'true Israel', whose mission was to inspire others in their adoration of Yahweh and bring them back to the ways of the Lord.

It is to these people that this prophecy speaks, those whom God had formed 'in the womb to be his servant to bring Jacob back to him and gather Israel to himself' (Isaiah 49:5). They knew what God wanted of them, and invested all their energy towards this end, the full restoration of Israel as a nation, with all its religious apparatus focused on the temple which would surely be rebuilt. They lived for the day when they could return to the 'promised land', to see their purpose fulfilled, and it seemed that Isaiah was confirming their convictions.

But the prophecy does not stop there. With this great and glorious task in mind, this supreme goal for the 'servant of the LORD', God carries on speaking thus:

It is too small a thing for you to be my servant
    to restore the tribes of Jacob
    and bring back those of Israel I have kept.
I will also make you a light for the Gentiles,
    that you may bring my salvation to the ends of the earth. (v. 6)

Through Isaiah's prophecy Yahweh reveals his heart to his servant: 'Don't you understand? It is good that you want to restore your people. I also want them to be faithful to me, and for them to be raised up again. But I will *never* be satisfied with that. Yes, I want Israel to know me, but my purpose for you cannot be limited to that and nothing more. There is a world which needs to know me, which needs to see the light I have put in you. If you don't give it to them, they will stay in darkness, and if you don't offer them the salvation I have given you, they will remain dead. The nations, oh my child, the nations – even those nations where I have taken you, your cruel conquerors. But not only there – those faraway empires you've heard rumours of; they also need me. You are their light. Let it shine on them, to the far shores and the distant peoples.'

The loving heart of God for the whole world which does not yet know him beats through Isaiah's words. Again we understand that God has blessed his people so that they in turn can be a blessing for all the families of the earth. However, there is another shade of meaning which does not come through when we read this passage in our Bibles.

In Isaiah 49:6, 'too small a thing' is the translation of the Hebrew word *qalal*, a term used 82 times in the Bible. Its Strong number is 07043, in case anyone wants to do their own study on *qalal*. It has a meaning which goes much further than 'too small' or 'insignificant'. But before we take a look at some of the other places where it is used and see how it is translated, it is worth mentioning one other factor which needs to be taken into account when doing a study of this nature.

The Old Testament was written over a period of around

1,000 years, during which time Hebrew as a language evolved. Not only were new words incorporated, but the meanings of words themselves also changed. This is not actually so surprising if we consider the history of the English language. Many words now mean something completely different from what they meant just 400 years ago when the King James version of the Bible (AV) was first produced, for example. When speaking of 'the quick and the dead', pedestrians on a zebra crossing are not what is in mind! In the seventeenth century, 'quick' simply meant 'living'. We have already seen the meaning of the Greek word *agape* in New Testament times, referring to the selfless giving love that God shows towards us. However, *agape* did not always carry that meaning. In the Septuagint, for example, it is used extensively in Song of Songs, where it refers to erotic love. So, too, in Hebrew words can and do change their meanings. We must therefore not take for granted that a word has kept the same meaning over time, and be careful never to project past meanings artificially onto later uses. In the case of *qalal*, the word has in fact maintained the same meaning, and the following selection, given in the order they appear in the Bible, gives something of an idea of the breadth of meaning the word contains.

After the flood, Yahweh states that he will not *curse* the ground again (Genesis 8:21). In Genesis 12:3, God promises Abraham that he will bless those who bless him, and *curse* those who *curse* him. In chapter 16 of the same book, verses 4 and 5, Hagar *despised* Sarai. The Mosaic Law ordered that he who *curses* his father or mother should be killed (Exodus 21:17). The book of Leviticus states that the blasphemer – that is, the person who has *cursed* God – should be stoned

(Leviticus 24:14, 23). Eli's sons were judged by God because they *made themselves vile* or *accursed* (1 Samuel 3:13). After dancing before the ark of the covenant, David promised Michal that he would make himself yet *more vile* in her eyes in order to praise God (2 Samuel 6:22).When they faced the soldiers of Judah, the men of Israel accused them of having *despised* them when they took the decision to bring the king back (2 Samuel 19:43). Jeroboam and all Israel together with him asked Rehoboam, when he began his reign, to *make* his yoke *lighter* upon them, though he refused (1 Kings 12:4, 9–10). In Isaiah's prophecy over Tyre, we see God acting to *bring into contempt* its pride (Isaiah 23:9). Jeremiah reproached the leaders of Israel for healing the hurt of the people *slightly* (Jeremiah 6:14). Ezekiel asks the people if it is a *light thing* for the house of Judah to be committing the abominations they are committing (Ezekiel 8:17).

There is another derivative of *qalal* which is used in the Scriptures: *q'lalah*, which means exclusively 'curse' or 'accursed'. Among other places, it is used in Genesis 27:12, where Jacob fears that he will receive his father's curse for trying to deceive him, and in Deuteronomy 11:26, when Moses places a path of blessing or of curse before the people of Israel. With all this in mind, I think we can begin to 'feel' something of the meaning of *qalal*.[1]

---

[1] To do complete justice to the subject, we would really need to look at the verb tense and mood used in each reference, seeing as this does change the meaning somewhat, but at least we have gained an overall impression of this Hebrew term. For those who would like a few more details, I would just say here that *qalal* in Isaiah 49 is in the 'Niphal' form, this being the reflexive or passive of the simple verb form known as 'Qal', which is used in Genesis 16:4, for example. Genesis 12:3 uses the 'Piel'

So what is it that God is saying to his servant, the remnant of Israel, in Isaiah 49:6? Can we not hear more clearly now the heart cry of God? He was longing for them to stop thinking first of themselves, and pay attention to the nations of the world. 'Listen, Israel. Stop thinking about yourself all the time. Compared to the magnitude of my desire to bring salvation to all the nations of the world, your restoration is a small thing, insignificant, petty, worthless and despised. Listen to my heart! I desire my bride from every tribe, tongue, people and nation, and your self-centred wish to be blessed becomes a curse if it is not channelled into blessing for those around you. Oh Israel! Forget what seems important to you and give yourselves to the nations.'

Years later the nationalist Pharisee Saul, converted into the apostle Paul, would hear God's mandate for his life expressed in this very text (see Acts 13:47). It was not written for him, but through his meditation on the Word, the Spirit of God applied it to his life and he responded in obedience to his new Lord. The simple desire of God, expressed in his Word, was converted into a commandment for Paul, and that's how it should be for every believer today. A 'Hebrew of Hebrews', Paul turned his back on his own people, who also needed God, to take the gospel to the despised Gentiles; a decision which cost him dearly. He had understood the heart of God and had put to one side his intense and justifiable desire to see the people of God restored; a desire to which Romans 9 gives eloquent testimony. And all

---

form, which denotes an intensification of the simple verb form; 'curse' is thus the intentional and stronger form of 'make light' or 'despise'. However, as can be seen, all share a very related meaning.

to dedicate himself completely to satisfying the desire of God to see his salvation reach the ends of the earth.

And today? What would the Lord say to us about our plans for new buildings costing millions? About our 'small ambitions' to be somebody within our denomination or nation? Of our evangelistic strategies to plant our denomination where it doesn't yet exist, despite the fact that there are 36 other churches in the same town? Of our interminable round of 'revival' conferences without which we wouldn't know how to survive? About the unbalanced perspective of our church members who only call a meeting 'good' if they have 'received a blessing'? About our real preoccupations and longings? About the poverty of our true commitment to mission?

What is it that motivates us in the Lord's church today? Do we not also need to give the Lord a chance to speak about our projects and ideas? Should it not be urgent for us to seek *his* priorities for his church? Our lives have been contaminated by selfishness and ethnocentricity, and the church has fallen prisoner to this way of thinking, until it has become dominated by an 'ecclesiocentric' outlook which destroys our effective testimony to the unreached nations of the world.

Let's learn to 'count ourselves as nothing', to 'consider worthless' and even 'despise' our own objectives, if only God would consider us worthy to extend his kingdom among the nations of the world. Our time has come, and it is not the time for getting so fat that we fall over and can't move under the weight of blessing that has been poured out on us. It is time to listen to the heart cry of God, to discover what is really important to him, and to make our decisions based on what we hear.

Are we in concordance?

14

Something Old, Something New

It looked like an interesting book: *New Testament Order for Church and Missionary*. Just what I needed on setting out for the 'mission field'. And indeed it was very interesting – a complete manual on 'New Testament methods for planting New Testament churches'. But what took me aback most was the enormous number of differences I found on comparing it with what I had learned in my own church, which also claimed to be based on New Testament teaching about the church.

I had begun to attend that church when I came back from abroad, where I had come to faith in Christ. It was an independent, charismatic church, in many ways similar to all the other new churches which were springing up in England during the 1970s and 80s. But in some respects this one was different. The women wore long skirts and veils (well, more like veils, hats, scarves, handkerchiefs, caps, boaters and bonnets – a veritable catwalk of millinery fashion). Women did not preach either, although they were allowed to give testimonies of 15 or 20 minutes which included Scripture references. And although we sang and clapped to the latest choruses with their lively rhythms, there was certainly no dancing – nothing more, in fact, than restrained foot-tapping, in marked contrast to many charismatic churches at the time where 'dancing in the Spirit' was the order of the day.

When I asked why, they told me that this was what the New Testament taught about women, and they didn't dance because there was no mention of dancing in the church in the New Testament. Didn't David dance before the ark of the covenant? And didn't Miriam, Moses' sister, lead the women in a dance to celebrate God's victory? 'Yes,' they replied, 'but that was in the old covenant; in the new one there's no dancing.'

Old or New, ancient or modern, old fashioned, out of step and obsolete, or relevant for today. This is how we treat the two 'Testaments' which make up our Bibles. We divide the Word of God into two, and between Malachi and Matthew we have inserted a blank page, usually bearing the title 'New Testament', just to make it absolutely clear. But beware – this page is not inspired by God either.

There certainly was an old covenant, which – thankfully! – has now been superseded by the new covenant in Christ. We are thus free from the burden of the civic and ceremonial demands found in the covenant God made with the nation of Israel that overshadowed so much of their life, and can worship God with the freedom that is ours in Christ. This much I gladly acknowledge. But we have unwittingly gone too far in our rejection of the old covenant – we have wrongly identified the new covenant which Jesus was to make on behalf of the new people of God with the body of the Greek New Testament writings, and abandoned the witness of the 'Old Testament' as pertaining purely to a bygone era, that of the old covenant. The fact that both 'covenant' and 'testament' can translate the same Greek word (*diatheke*) must not be allowed to lead us into confusion; the old covenant may well be the out-of-date covenant, but the Old Testament most certainly is not the out-of-date Word of God. It does need to be read in the light of its prophetic fulfilment found in Christ, but it still needs to be read.

In everything we say and do we demonstrate a neglect of the 'Old' Testament and its message. Few believers have read all of it, fewer read it regularly, and even fewer know how to interpret it correctly. With a simple 'We aren't under the law, we're under grace', we discard in one go the Word of God transmitted to his people during around 1,000 years, which makes up 80 per cent of our Bibles. And even worse, if that were possible, we attribute to the Lord Jesus attitudes towards the Hebrew-Aramaic Scriptures that are unthinkable. In spite of his crystal-clear words in the Sermon on the Mount in Matthew 5:17–18, where he tells us, 'Do not think that I have come to do away with the Law of Moses and the teachings of the prophets. . .' (GNB), we teach that he cancels out the Law in favour of his own interpretation and application of divine principles.

In doing this we come dangerously close to the second-century heresies of Marcion, who did not accept that the God of the Old Testament was the same as the God whom Jesus revealed in the New. Consequently he rejected the entire Old Testament, and anything from the New Testament which had to do with the traditions of the Jews. As you can imagine, he was left with a very slim Bible. Perhaps we don't tear out the pages, but we are just the same in the minimum amount of attention we pay to its content.

We publish the 'New' on its own, as if it could be understood without the background of the 'Old'. However, I've never seen a modern edition of the Old Testament without the New, unless it was a Jewish Bible which recognises neither Jesus nor his 'New Testament'. The edition of the Bible I was given on going to secondary school even printed certain parts of the Mosaic Law in smaller print, in three columns instead of two; not because they are less important, oh no, of course not, but to save space, and to be able to offer this edition at a more accessible price.

We protect ourselves behind a few favourite scriptures, from the New Testament of course, and taken out of context. For example, 'But now . . . we have been released from the law so that we serve in the new way of the Spirit, and not in the old way of the written code' (Romans 7:6). Or, 'By calling this covenant "new", he has made the first one obsolete; and what is obsolete and ageing will soon disappear' (Hebrews 8:13). Or again, 'He has made us competent as ministers of a new covenant – not of the letter but of the Spirit; for the letter kills, but the Spirit gives life' (2 Corinthians 3:6).

By doing this we relegate to a level of spiritual mediocrity the real experience of God that David had, or even Moses, or the people of God under the spiritual leadership of Hezekiah. And in fact all we end up doing is showing our ignorance of the difference between 'law' and 'legalism', of the role that the Law of Moses played in the worship of the believers in former times, and of the real content of the 'gospel'. (Whether we like it or not, the message of the 'gospel' also existed in the days of Abraham and Moses, according to Galatians 3:8 and Hebrews 4:2 at any rate. This was not a

Christ-centred gospel, true, and lacked the fundamental clarity that came to the preaching of the message of the kingdom of God with the death and crucifixion of the Lord Jesus Christ. But it was nevertheless there; let us not forget that it was an Old Testament prophet who first told us that 'the righteous will live by their faith' [Habakkuk 2:4 NLT].) It seems to me that in many of our churches today we are languishing beneath the same yoke of pharisaical, barren legalism, despite living under the ministry of the Holy Spirit.

What is the Old Testament good for? We have the Psalms, which are good for every occasion. And Isaiah, of course; a delightful book. Then there are some stories which are especially good for our little ones in the Sunday school, such as David and Goliath, or crossing the Red Sea. It's also a good source of illustrations for our sermons, and it provides us with many characters worthy of study: Gideon, Samson, Deborah (although we have to be careful with this last one, as we wouldn't want her getting mixed up in our doctrine on women in leadership according to the New Testament, would we?). In summary, a collection of bits and pieces which can be used to support the central, fundamental message which is to be found, without a doubt, in the New Testament. There really are very few people who show any capacity, or even desire, to listen to God in any serious, organised way through the pages of the Old Testament.

Where has this led us? To our shame, we have created a 'scaled-down' gospel, and have lost the incalculable riches of an understanding of those Scriptures which were the Bible of the early church. The New Testament was never meant to replace the Old, but to complement it, built up on the ethical and religious foundation that the latter provides. The central doctrines of Christianity have their roots in the Old Testament, not in the teaching of the apostles. The New Testament takes as read the teaching of the Old, and does not repeat it, and we will never understand the mind of God without putting the Old Testament in the place it deserves. As such, it is impossible for us ever to become mature, balanced Christians if we do not dedicate ourselves to understanding and applying the message revealed throughout both Testaments, and not just the New as we are accustomed to do, with a bit of help from the Old.

For New Testament church leaders the Old Testament was the basis for their sermons and teaching. Their quiet times were spent in the book of Leviticus! Gradually, as the New Testament writings began to circulate, these were added, bringing accurate information about the life, death and resurrection of the Lord Jesus, and apostolic application of teaching to real-life first-century situations. But the ethical foundation for godly Christian living was still found in the Old Testament. Once we have learned to sift through the ceremonial injunctions which were abrogated at Christ's death, we find a real treasure trove of guidelines for living and teaching. The Ten Commandments, for example, continue even today to provide a powerful bedrock for human society for those who care to take the time to unpack them and apply them. Old Testament case law provides numerous examples of how one specific society could apply these, avoiding 'the letter of the law' yet obeying the spirit it transmits. Modern 'moral relativity', whether in the realm of sexual ethics, religious truth or business practices, finds its counterpoint in Old Testament teaching. The church that finds itself 'at sea' today is the one that has lost the anchor of a right understanding of Old Testament ethics.

We would do well to take to heart the comment that Jesus made when he asked his disciples if they understood his teaching. When they answered in the affirmative, he added, 'Therefore every teacher of the law who has been instructed about the kingdom of heaven is like the owner of a house who brings out of his storeroom new treasures as well as old' (Matthew 13:52). We need to embrace everything new that comes with the revelation of the gospel, but in no way throw out the old, former things. We need to learn how to keep both in perfect harmony.

It falls outside the scope of this book to treat this subject in the necessary depth, or to give guidelines for the interpretation of the Old Testament which would enable us to understand and apply it correctly, but I do encourage readers to seek out the resources to be able to do this. It's worth it, and very much so. I will limit myself here to exploring one of the effects of ignoring the Old Testament in the loss of the broad biblical basis for missions which it offers.

How do we justify the missionary efforts of the church from the Bible? Most believers open their Bibles at the so-called Great Commission and quote Jesus. So far so good, but what else? 'Well, there must be one or two other verses, but not many. And you shouldn't base your teaching on one single verse, right?' And then we know, or we think we know, that Jesus was sent only to the 'lost sheep of Israel', and we feel justified in doing the same. We stick to our own, convinced that God will send others as missionaries. And, almost without realising it, we consign the whole subject of missions to one department of the church, and it ceases to be its driving force, its very reason for being.

But what does the Old Testament teach on this subject? Isn't it the story of a rebellious people who were never obedient to God? And what does it teach us about missions if we know that they were a people who did not want to share the blessing of God with the nations, who made themselves the exclusive owners of the universal God, and never offered to other peoples what God in his goodness had given to them? We read the Old Testament through a filter, seeing only the disobedience of the people and skipping over the Word of God which was revealed to them. The very same criticisms could be levelled at the church today, but that does not mean that we have not received a clear missions mandate.

From Genesis to Malachi the Old Testament is full of references which reveal God's purpose for his world and how he chose a people for himself; not chosen for their own merits but so that they could be a source of blessing to all the nations of the earth. The disobedience of Israel in no way invalidates this revelation. Indeed, what it does is put this responsibility firmly at the feet of the church, the people grafted onto the olive tree which is Israel, in order to fulfil God's purpose for the nations – a purpose which was neglected by the natural Israel.

The Bible opens with the declaration of the universality of Yahweh, Creator and Protector of all humanity. God cannot be limited to one stretch of land in the Middle East, nor to an idolatrous image which ties his worship irredeemably to one geographical area. The old Law revealed to Moses conclusively prohibits idolatry, with the intention of preserving the universal nature of the worship of Yahweh.

God is the author of cultural, linguistic and racial diversity. Genesis 10, a chapter known as the 'table of the nations', relates the creation of the first human nations, descendants of one father, but dispersed by God after the incident of the tower of Babel. It informs us about the descendants of the sons of Noah, 'by their clans and languages, in their territories and nations . . . From these the nations spread out over the earth after the flood' (Genesis 10:31–32). In this moment the seeds were sown for all the ethnic variety we know today. These are the nations God has in mind when he calls Abraham, in order that he receive his blessing, and so that through him 'all peoples on earth will be blessed' (Genesis 12:3).

The blessing of Abraham contains three basic elements: the fact that he will become a great nation, a land for this blessed people to dwell in, and the message of salvation through which all the other nations of the earth will be blessed. The first two elements existed to give 'logistical support' to the realisation of the third, but they were never meant to be ends in themselves. However, as the years passed Israel began to undervalue this divine task in favour of their identity as a nation and their national security. Under the rule of an earthly king they abandoned the pure worship of Yahweh in their efforts to be just like their neighbours, descending into the abyss of idolatry, temple prostitution and human sacrifice. In their desire to 'be someone' in the ranking of the nations, they lost the holiness which should have been their hallmark, and sacrificed the message of salvation for all on the altar of their own pride.

However, God proceeded to re-establish his priorities for them, leaving his people at the mercy of fierce and relentless nations, reducing them to an historical low and ejecting them from the land he himself had given them. Why? Not for their sakes, that much is clear, but for the testimony which he wanted to make reach the ends of the earth. He wanted to cleanse the land of the disgraceful things his people had done, engaging 'in all the detestable practices of the nations the LORD had driven out before the Israelites' (1 Kings 14:24), and begin to undo the damage done by the sins of Israel. He wanted the nations to know that he was God. Although they speak of a future time, the words of Isaiah echo this sentiment:

> I will set a sign among them and I will send some of those who survive to the nations . . . and to the distant islands that have not heard of my fame or seen my glory. They will proclaim my glory among the nations. (Isaiah 66:19)

Seventy years after the beginning of the exile, when he reunited a remnant of Israel from among the nations where they had been dispersed, he did not do it for love of them. Once again the primary motive of God's actions is the testimony of his glory before the nations:

> What I am going to do is not for the sake of you Israelites, but for the sake of my holy name, which you have disgraced in every country where you have gone. When I demonstrate to the nations the holiness of my great name – the name you disgraced among them – then they will know that I am the LORD. I, the Sovereign LORD, have spoken. (Ezekiel 36:22–23 GNB)

Even the return of this minority to the promised land was intended to demonstrate to the nations that Yahweh was

God, capable of doing what was impossible in their eyes, and worthy of being worshipped by all.

Between these two moments in history – the commission of Abraham (and through him, of all Israel) and the establishing of Israel once again in Palestine after the exile – the Old Testament is the story of God's desire to bless his people, so that in turn they could become a channel of blessing for the peoples of the world. It is a constant struggle against the human tendency to selfishness and ethnocentrism. But there it is. Time after time we meet a God who wants to mould his people into a vehicle capable of taking his message to the nations, and a people who seem to be interested only in self-glorification.

It is a story full of moments of desperation, when all seems to be lost. One of those is the reign of Manasseh, who led Israel 'astray, so that they did more evil than the nations the LORD had destroyed before the Israelites' (2 Kings 21:9). The third chapter of Ezekiel is a masterpiece of reproach to Israel: God is disgusted with his people and out of the mouth of his prophet he pours out on them a tirade which even sinks to vulgarities (v. 20), their sin has reached such depths. 'Was it not enough that you should be a prostitute? Must you also slaughter my children by sacrificing them to idols?' he asks with evident anger (Ezekiel 16:20–21 NLT).

However, there are also some tremendously inspiring moments, when at least a few representatives of the pagan nations come to enjoy a living relationship with Yahweh. The exodus is an example of 'strategic spiritual warfare', as we would say today, when God executed his judgements on the gods of Egypt (Exodus 12:12), which resulted in the salvation of 'many people who were not Israelites' (Exodus

12:38 NLT), who accompanied them and became completely integrated in the life of that nation. On entering the promised land, Rahab is the first to be incorporated into Israel, and later even features in the genealogy of the Messiah, if we are dealing with the same Rahab (Matthew 1:5), which is more than likely.

There is another Gentile woman who features in the lineage of the Lord Jesus Christ: Ruth. She was not only a Gentile, but a Moabite. She had a genuine conversion, and was accepted among the Israelites despite the clear prohibition in Deuteronomy 23:3, 'No . . . Moabite or any of his descendants may enter the assembly of the LORD, even down to the tenth generation.' And we say that in Old Testament times they were legalistic. I wonder how many of *our* churches would have accepted her as a member. . .

In the Psalms we can find some of the clearest indications of the missionary consciousness of the nation of Israel. Yahweh is proclaimed in song as the sovereign King of all the earth (47:8), who will judge all the nations in justice (9:8), and who will be adored among the nations (22:27–28). Israel recognises her responsibility not only to praise him in her own meetings, but also before the nations (18:49), and, what is more, to proclaim him to all the peoples (105:1). The Psalms contain a direct evangelistic message (47:1), and include prayers for the fulfilment of God's promise with regard to the nations (72:19). Psalms 96 and 67 are examples of two extremely 'missionary' psalms, representative of the sentiments behind the whole book.

Although they had little choice but to direct their attention to the sin of their own nation, the prophets also demonstrate a desire to make their God known among the nations. Chapter after chapter is dedicated to messages of correction and rebuke for their sin, calling them to surrender themselves to Yahweh, the only true God (for example, Isaiah 13–21, 23; Jeremiah 47–51; Ezekiel 25–32 and the whole of Daniel and Nahum, among other passages scattered throughout the prophets). And what about Jonah, a book dedicated to the love of God towards the most important city on the earth at that time? Jonah was not an exemplary missionary, but that's not the point – it is a book about the revelation of God's heart for the nations. And Daniel even includes a whole chapter written by a pagan king, convicted and converted to the worship of Yahweh, but not a Jew – Nebuchadnezzar is ostensibly the author of chapter 4.

When in Malachi the curtain falls for the last time on the prophetic voice of God in the Old Testament, God is still not happy when he looks at the commitment of his people. 'Oh, that one of you would shut the temple doors, so that you would not light useless fires on my altar! I am not pleased with you . . . and I will accept no offering from your hands.' But he is able to add, 'In every place incense and pure offerings will be brought to my name, because my name will be great among the nations . . . But you profane it' (Malachi 1:10–12). Israel is still preoccupied with herself and seems incapable of changing, but the name of God has been glorified among the nations.

And we say that there is no missionary message in the Old Testament! Perhaps we don't read in so many words, 'Listen, O Israel – you ought to go out and evangelise the nations, and make an effort to put your faith in context so that all the nations can take part together with you in the blessing of knowing me.' But the message is there, visible through the pages of the history of a people who did not want to be a vessel of the blessing of God to other nations.

And what about us? What motivates us? Larger numbers in the congregation? Guarding the borders of our particular bit of 'promised land'? Maintaining our style of worship even if the heart has gone out of it? Or being a blessing to the nations of the earth? Are we willing to be a vessel, whatever price we may have to pay? 'Lord, bless us so that the nations can receive from you through us.'

I'll tell you a secret: I've seen the end of the film; I know how the story ends. There, in that tremendous atmosphere of worship rising up to him who is seated on the throne and to the Lamb throughout all eternity, there will be representatives of every language, every nation, every tribe, every people. They'll all be there. The nations will know our God.

There's no question about God's plan being fulfilled or not; what's uncertain is our participation in it. God will be glorified; about that there can be no doubt. The question is how. 'Now all this is an example for us' (1 Corinthians 10:6 GNB): in the Old Testament we have the example of Israel, chosen for a purpose which she did not fulfil. And God had to raise up others, you and me, to complete the task. Let's learn from the 'old things', ask God to infuse our hearts with his priorities, and we will fulfil his desire to see his glory extended among the nations.

15

'Let Us Eat and Drink, for Tomorrow We Die'

I am sure that you know the old anecdote about the man who was looking for guidance from God. In good evangelical style, he turned to the Word of God, but then closed his eyes in prayer for a few moments and opened his Bible at random. He placed the tip of his finger on some place on the open page, hoping to find the guidance he so desperately needed. . .

'Then Judas went and hanged himself,' the text said.

'Oooh, I wonder what the Lord wants to say to me with that one? Let's try again.'

After another quick prayer, once again he opened his Bible, and once again he pointed his finger at an open page.

'Go and do likewise.'

'Oh my God! Surely you don't want me to . . . do you? Please give me some confirmation.'

Now more than a bit frightened, this poor believer went through his ceremony for getting divine guidance once again. The reply was dreadfully clear. 'What you have to do, do it quickly.'

As can be seen in this apocryphal story, it is one thing to declare that the Bible is the inspired and infallible Word of God, but quite another to know how to understand it, interpret it and apply it in a correct way. Many declare the Bible to be inspired, but those who know how to give a right application of this inspired Word in the situations in which we live today are few and far between. Of course the Bible is inspired by God, but what does it mean? In what ways can it be used? Under what circumstances may we legitimately exclaim with faith and joy, 'Let us eat and drink, for tomorrow we die!' (Isaiah 22:13)? And just how are we supposed to take certain declarations we find in the Scriptures?

For example, the Bible contains some of Satan's own words. 'All this I will give you if you kneel down and worship me,' are words spoken by Satan to the Lord Jesus. Are we supposed to believe that these words on the devil's lips were inspired by God? Or is it rather the fact that they are included in the Word of God that is inspired?

Then we have some of the words spoken by Job's 'bosom buddies' – and with friends like that, who needs enemies? Some of the things they come out with are absolute monstrosities. In a true display of sensitivity and compassion at another's suffering, Bildad says, 'Your children must have sinned against God, and so he punished them as they deserved' (Job 8:4 GNB – also in the rest of this chapter). Zofar seems to wish Job even greater misfortune when he says, 'God is punishing you less than you deserve' (Job 11:6). Elifaz also shows how little he understands God's thoughts about Job when he assures him, 'Your wickedness is evident by what you say; you are trying to hide behind clever words. There is no need for me to condemn you; you are condemned by every word you speak' (Job 15:5–6). To crown it all, Elihu wipes the floor with Job:

> Have you ever seen anyone like this man Job?
> He never shows respect for God.
> He likes the company of evil people
> and goes about with sinners. . .
> Any sensible person will surely agree;
> and the wise who hear me will say
> that Job is speaking from ignorance
> and that nothing he says makes sense.
> Think through everything that Job says;
> you will see that he talks like an evil man.
> To his sins he adds rebellion;
> in front of us all he mocks God.
> (Job 34:7–8, 35–37)

All of these statements are 'biblical', and undoubtedly inspired by God, since they can be found on the pages of the Bible. But in no way can we consider that their *content* is 'inspired', or that they represent 'inspired' thoughts or attitudes. To tell the truth, in the case of Job's friends' comments, these directly contradict what God spoke to Satan in the first chapter: 'Did you notice my servant Job? There is no one on earth as faithful and good as he is. He worships me and is careful not to do anything evil' (Job 1:8). These comments are rather the product of faulty human reasoning, and are found in the biblical record to teach us how *not* to think, act and speak.

When we learn to read the Bible in this way we find numerous texts which reveal much more about the speaker's state of heart than about God's will for us. The devil and Job's friends are not the only ones who make their mark with highly 'uninspired' feelings contained in wholly 'inspired' passages.

Let's look at the godly discipline exercised by Nehemiah in the course of his leadership: 'I reprimanded the men, called down curses on them, beat them, and pulled out their hair' (Nehemiah 13:25). Is this an example that all good Christian leaders today should imitate? Then there is Aaron, another outstanding leader in Israel. In a moment of supreme theological madness, or maybe just political expedience, he made the Israelites a golden calf and promised them a 'festival to honour the Lord' at which they could all shout, 'Israel, this is our god, who led us out of Egypt!' (Exodus 32:1–5). Or what about the depth of commitment to God that Jacob shows when he promises God, 'If you will be with me and protect me on the journey I am making and give me food and clothing, and if I return safely to my father's home, then you will be my God' (Genesis 28:20–21). His generosity towards his Creator is boundless.

So, we see that all the Bible is inspired, but that does not give us the right to extract sentences or phrases from it and claim that they represent God's thoughts. On the contrary, each phrase must be considered within its context and the purpose for which it is included in the Bible. With this in mind, let us turn to the Psalms.

The Psalms, indeed. That book of prayer and praise that is so highly valued by believers of all times and places. It is the 'Christian hymnbook' that was written not by Isaac Watts or Charles Wesley, nor by any of the other great composers of hymns through church history, but rather by God himself. (In fact, for many years various Christian traditions did not allow the use of any 'worship' that was not from the psalms themselves, preferring songs penned by God rather than others that were merely 'human'.) Many believers find comfort and strength in their verses. So many of us have received an injection of trust from that most famous of psalms, Psalm 23, or have enjoyed the security which another psalm can bring us:

> He will cover you with his wings;
> you will be safe in his care;
> his faithfulness will protect and defend you.
> You need not fear. . .
> A thousand may fall dead beside you,
> ten thousand all round you,
> but you will not be harmed.
> (Psalm 91:4–5, 7)

The psalms are considered as 'model prayers', definitely 'inspired', which guide believers in expressing themselves to God.

But only about a third of the psalms can be considered psalms of 'trust'. The majority are rather expressions of anguish, pain, conflict, suffering, injustice, the desire for vengeance, or feelings of distance from God. How are these imprecatory psalms to be understood? Can they also be used as model prayers? When I suffer injustice at the hands of a neighbour or a manager, can I make the psalmist's words mine, when he says, 'Strike them with blindness! Make their backs always weak!' or, 'May red-hot coals fall on them; may they be thrown into a pit and never get out' (Psalm 69:23; 140:10)?

What should we do with statements like these? Can they

be read in the same way that we read the 'nicer' psalms; in other words, as expressions of God's heart? Or are they rather the outbursts of hurting and frightened people? When considered against the backdrop of biblical revelation as a whole, including the forgiveness and mercy that God wants his people to show, even to their enemies, we cannot consider these as 'acceptable' prayers to God. Nevertheless, here they are, part of an inspired Bible.

Perhaps the best way to understand these psalms is as one very real facet of prayer – an individual's struggles with his circumstances, calling out to God, and giving vent to the deepest feelings that torment his inner being. Anything goes in God's presence – anger (against anyone and everyone, including God himself), impotence, anguish, rejoicing and desperation. All in all both sides of human experience. We all experience 'not nice' emotions, and as believers we can and must have complete freedom to pour out our hearts, however putrid they may be, before our God.

Another example. Theologically speaking, we all know that God has said to us, 'I will never leave you; I will never abandon you' (Hebrews 13:5 – and the Greek uses a 'double negative' construction which could perhaps be better translated, 'No, I will never ever leave you; I will never ever abandon you'). God is with us, and we do not doubt it. Nevertheless, there are times when our heart feels an enormous void within, as if God were a million light years from this planet and, on top of this, as if we were less important to him than the most insignificant little worm. At times like that we make the psalmist's words our own: 'Why are you so far away, O Lord? Why do you hide yourself when we are in trouble?' (Psalm 10:1), or, in even more daring words, 'How much longer will you forget me, LORD? Forever? How much longer will you hide yourself from me?' (Psalm 13:1).

In reality God is never far away – but there are times in our experience when he is, or at least when it feels like that to us. We cannot allow the 'inspired' nature of these psalms to bring us to claim that God really had abandoned the psalmist, or us. Of course not. Rather, the inspiration in these passages is found in the fact that God, in his tremendous goodness to us, allows us in this way to share the struggles of saints of old, in order that their frankness and importunity in calling out to God may inspire something of the same honesty and transparency in us. Of course these psalms were inspired by God, but as a revelation of the depths of the human heart, and not as indications of God's supreme desire for humanity.

Let us now turn to one specific psalm, which will also bring us a little closer to the central theme of this book – Psalm 137. It is a psalm which sensitive readers find repugnant, and which, until we understand this particular 'inspiration' of the psalms, is utterly meaningless. Its final verse has given more than one reader a big headache – and rightly so. How can verse 9 – 'Happy are those . . . who take your babies and smash them against a rock' – represent what God desires for a people who have not understood his grace?

Before we try to understand more clearly what this verse may have to teach us with its agonising cry for vengeance, let us read the full psalm in its context, and in so doing somehow get inside the skin of its authors, and feel their pain-filled history:

By the rivers of Babylon we sat down;
  there we wept when we remembered Zion.
On the willows near by
  we hung up our harps.
Those who captured us told us to sing;
  they told us to entertain them:
  'Sing us a song about Zion.'
How can we sing a song to the LORD
  in a foreign land?
May I never be able to play the harp again
  if I forget you, Jerusalem!
May I never be able to sing again
  if I do not remember you,
  if I do not think of you as my greatest joy!
Remember, LORD, what the Edomites did
  the day Jerusalem was captured.
Remember how they kept saying,
  'Tear it down to the ground!'
Babylon, you will be destroyed.
Happy are those who pay you back
  for what you have done to us –
  who take your babies
  and smash them against a rock.

'Happy are those . . . who take your babies and smash them against a rock.' What on earth could have brought the people of God to the point of wishing that on their enemies? Without for one moment seeking to justify such barbarous attitudes, what were the experiences that led the worship singers of Israel to cry out in hatred instead of joyfully singing the 'songs of Zion'; what led them to fill their 'psalms' – vehicles of praise to Yahweh – with blood-curdling calls for vengeance?

As we have seen in previous chapters, the people of Israel had got bogged down in matters relating to the maintenance of their nation as a state, and had lost sight of *why* they had received God's blessing. But God's purposes will not be frustrated, and he had allowed the unthinkable: barbarous nations, ferocious, unjust and wicked warrior states, had swept over Israel and wiped it out. First the northern tribes, at the hands of the Assyrians, and then Judah, when conquered by the Babylonian empire, had fallen under the sway of Gentile kingdoms.

Now – and let us be clear about this – there was nothing 'genteel' in 'Gentile' conquests. Wars in those days were not fought according to the rules of a 'just war' that are supposed to be followed in armed conflicts these days, or at least those involving the 'civilised' nations of the West. (What a Utopia! To think that to kill and maim, to squash a people until they surrender at the feet of a more powerful conqueror, to sow panic among the fragments of shrapnel and human remains that go flying through the air . . . that all this can be carried out according to some 'gentlemen's agreement'. How naïve we are. It seems that we have not understood just how deeply sin has penetrated the human heart.)

Wars are horrendous, and they always have been. Histories of blood, death, separation, oppression, treason, rape and destruction. And the fall of the kingdoms of Israel and Judah was no different. No doubt Hosea's bloody prophecy against the northern kingdom would have been fulfilled: 'Samaria must be punished for rebelling against me. Her people will die in war; babies will be dashed to the ground, and pregnant women will be ripped open' (Hosea 13:16).

172 NOT EVERYTHING IN OUR BIBLES

It would have been no different for the nation of Judah. One hundred and fifty years earlier the Assyrians, as was their custom, had left a pyramid of severed heads at the entrance to Lachish to warn those who might have been tempted to rebellion or resistance. And they were defeated in the siege of Jerusalem only by God's direct intervention (see Isaiah 37). But this time there was no eleventh-hour deliverance. God's judgement, announced by Jeremiah and graphically foreseen by Habakkuk, was carried out. The 'holy city' fell, its wall was destroyed, and the temple furnishings were taken to Babylon. Most of the population would suffer the same fate as their Israelite compatriots earlier, apart from the small remnant who escaped to Egypt, those who were left to till the ground, and the rest who were taken off into captivity to Babylon.

There, seated 'by the rivers of Bablyon', the few survivors tried to rebuild their broken lives and community. But cataclysms of this nature don't just fade away into the past as if nothing had happened. In such circumstances it is hard to draw a line over the past and start again, as it were. As psychologists tell us, any catastrophe leaves its mark on its victims, who may suffer nightmares for years, or irrational anxiety, vividly reliving the tragedy. Those who had seen the brains of their little ones bashed out against the walls of their houses, the wombs of their pregnant wives or daughters ripped open with rough swords, and the vast majority of their families and friends lying lifeless among the remains of the ransacked city, now had to live among these murderers.

To cap it all, now they were being asked to sing some 'nice choruses', all happy-clappy, but in honour of the

Babylonian gods. How dare they? How *could* a Jew forget what had happened? So they called down all sorts of curses on themselves to relive even more intensely their pain and deprivation.

And what about those pagan barbarians? Let them rot! Let them go to 'the place they deserve'! And then, just like the family members of the suicide bombers who jump for joy as they see the dismembered bodies of Jews strewn over a market square in Tel Aviv, so they too would rejoice as soon as any other nation were able to conquer Babylon and in turn subject *them* to the same or even greater brutality. 'Happy are those . . . who take your babies and smash them against a rock.'

Now, let us not imagine that God approves of the attitudes that we see in the psalm. Its inclusion reveals to us how deeply hurt a human being can feel, and the strength of the desire for vengeance that this can create – a desire which obviously runs against the gospel of forgiveness. We see it in Simeon and Levi, when they deceive Shechem and his fellow citizens and then avenge the rape of their sister. We see it centuries later in Jonah, who would have preferred to see the destruction of Nineveh, capital of Israel's enemy, the Assyrian empire, rather than its repentance and restoration. We understand, and we may even consider this normal.

But God does not consider it 'normal', nor anything of the sort, and cannot just leave his people in this state of bitterness and angry resentment. He who cried out from the cross, 'Forgive them, Father! They don't know what they are doing,' wants to reproduce this same capacity in his people. He had a very different and higher purpose in bringing them to live among the nations, and little by little would heal them so that they could forgive, and even desire the best for their captors.

With time, this is precisely what happened. No doubt under the influence of Jeremiah's prophetic words (found in chapter 29, especially verses 4–7, 10–14), they started to take their place in the cities where they were held in captivity, and began to understand that God had placed them there to reveal his glory to the nations. The next psalm, 138, reveals something of the 180-degree about-turn which took place in the heart of the Jewish community in Babylon:

> I thank you, LORD, with all my heart;
>   I sing praise to you before the gods. . .
> All the kings in the world will praise you, LORD,
>   because they have heard your promises.
> They will sing about what you have done
>   and about your great glory.
> (Psalm 138:1, 4–5)

The Old Testament gives us no details of the people of Israel's recovery of their missionary vision, and we cannot affirm that this or any other highly 'missionary' psalms date from after this period. However, the results are tangible by the time we reach the New Testament period. Although there were still strong currents of resistance to the occupation of the promised land, many Jews, living in different cities across the Roman Empire, gave effective witness to the supremacy of their monotheistic worship of Yahweh. As we have seen, the book of Acts reflects this when speaking of the inclusion of many 'God-fearers' in Jewish worship in the synagogues. Missionary witness had emerged from the disaster of the exile, and the nations were being prepared for the preaching of the gospel of grace in Jesus Christ.

What does all this mean for us? We may never have suffered such tremendous misfortune as the people of God did in the sixth century BC. So we probably do not find the same attitudes so rooted in our hearts. However, if we are honest, we must recognise how strong our own ethnocentricity is, and how little we are concerned for the spread of the biblical message to the nations, especially those we consider 'different' or 'difficult'.

The Israelites suffered all this pain in their own flesh and blood, and gave free and indulgent expression to their resentment. But they also knew how to respond to God's insistent call, and became his spokesman to the nations. We have not suffered anything like this, but still keep ourselves aloof with our attitudes of superiority and contempt from peoples whose only sin is being different from us. Let us not forget that the murderer is not just the one who kills, but the one who refuses to give life. If the Lord sees the one who calls his brother a 'worthless fool' in the same light as a murderer, and the one who looks lustfully at a woman as if he had slept with her, then are we in fact so different from the people of Israel? Maybe we do not actually wish on anyone the same fate as that longed for by the psalmist, but when we refuse to allow the need of people across the world to break down the wall of our own indifference, and fail to provide them with the possibility of knowing the only message of salvation, are we in fact not consigning them to a far worse future?

Let us not fear to open our hearts in God's presence, and share with him the absolute worst things that we think and feel. But let us not stop there. Let us allow his Spirit to open new paths in our beings and in our churches, bringing us closer to nations who need what only we can give them – the gospel of forgiveness and grace in Jesus Christ. May rivers of blessing to the nations flow from the hardness of our hearts.

16

No Comment

We are coming to the end of our journey together through the pages of our Bibles. Much has already been said, but there is still one thing to comment on: the commentaries which often accompany our Bibles, especially the study versions. In the old days, Bibles came without any commentary at all; the text was 'pure', with just a few references at the foot of the page. But we are more modern, and it's not enough for us to have access to concordances, commentaries and reference books at home. We want to have as much as possible in with the biblical text.

The first one to become popular was the Scofield Bible, a great work complete with commentaries and biblical interpretations. It was followed by the Thompson Bible, another impressive tome, with an apparently endless amount of interesting information, especially useful to the pastor for producing an instant sermon. Biblical archaeology, chain references, outlines, key studies by character or theme, historical graphs . . . and all in one volume. It seemed that the bigger the Bible was, the more spiritual the preacher was –

the weight of the Bible was a conclusive measure of one's Christian stature. Pocket editions were reserved for those Christians who preferred to hide their light under a bushel, so to speak.

Since then a plethora of different study Bibles for all tastes and theological convictions has been produced, and the Scofield edition is reserved mainly for those believers of a dispensationalist persuasion, since this system of biblical interpretation is reflected in its notes. We have the Discipleship Bible (and as for the rest of us, what does that make us?), the Life Application Study Bible, at least one study edition for each different translation, the Pentecostal Study Bible, the Daily Bible, the Devotional Bible and the 'Jewish' Bible which preserves traces of the original language and Jewish tradition, among many others. Even the most simple Bible these days will normally have an introduction to the Bible itself, to both Testaments, and even to each book.

Now I know nobody claims that these helps contained in our Bibles are inspired. Thank the Lord, we have not yet reached the spiritual level of Joseph Smith, founder of the Mormons: to make the Bible fit better with his personal doctrines he published a 'corrected' version of the biblical text of the King James version, whose corrections were considered to be inspired. No. Our modern editions are all produced with the aim of helping us study the Bible by making available relevant information to enable us to understand better what we are reading. They are tools at our disposal to help us grow as believers, that's all.

They do not claim to impose an interpretation on the biblical text, but invariably that is what they end up doing. This

is especially the case in study Bibles with a particular doctrinal or denominational emphasis. Commenting on different verses, they present the interpretations of these verses
which are used as a basis for their theological position, usually without making any further comment. It is as if they
are saying, 'This is how we see it, and this is the definitive
meaning of this text or passage.' Very few present the alter-
natives offered by other branches of the body of Christ.

Even though we know that these comments do not form
part of the inspired text, the fact that they are found inside
the covers of our Bibles induces us to place too much faith
in their content, and we tend to read them without making
use of our critical faculties. 'If they've put it in the Bible, it
must be right, mustn't it? After all, the writer must be
somebody reliable, who knows about these things. That's
why he's the one who's writing it and I'm the one who's
reading it,' we think. It's rare for us to adopt the attitude of
the Bereans, who listened to the teaching of the apostle
Paul, but 'examined the scriptures every day to see if what
Paul said was true' (Acts 17:11).

We all allow ourselves to be influenced by others' teaching, and much more so if this teaching is presented together
with the Bible. We are fashioned not only by the Word of
God and the work of the Holy Spirit in our lives, but also by
the process of discipleship, in which we become imitators of
others. God has made us with a tremendous capacity for
absorbing what we see and hear in those around us. We are
'sponges' by nature. How many of us have seen the living
reflection of our worst habits in our children? What children do when they embark on the path of socialisation is
repeated by believers when they are born again. They

watch their family very closely, and adopt the traits of their brothers, sisters and parents in the faith.

It is a myth to think that we believe what we believe because we have studied and arrived at personal conclusions from a purely objective biblical perspective. Let's be honest. There are few of us who have taken the time to examine the foundations of our theological position, a task which would include taking a long look at the arguments of those who have arrived at different conclusions. And even when we do, it is not that easy to undo the foundations which have already been put into our Christian life. The commentaries in our Bibles can serve to reinforce these positions and so increase the distance between brothers and sisters in the body of Christ.

Why does a member of a Pentecostal church believe that speaking in tongues is the only sign of having been baptised in the Holy Spirit? Why does the renewed Presbyterian accept this gift, but not as a sign of a past experience? And why does a believer brought up on dispensationalism reject tongues completely? As Dr Jack Deere says in his book *Surprised by the Power of the Spirit*, 'Over the years, I have observed that the majority of what Christians believe is not derived from their own patient and careful study of the Scriptures. The majority of Christians believe what they believe because godly and respected teachers told them it was correct.'

Whether we like it or not, as a consequence of what we have been taught or what we have read, we develop a filter, or sieve, through which we read and interpret the Bible. It is extremely difficult for us to eliminate this filter, or even leave it aside for a limited period in order to be able to understand someone else's position, or to be able to do a somewhat less biased study of the Scriptures. However, it is of fundamental importance if we want to understand the Word of God, written to different people, with different mentalities, living in different times, and if we want to grow in our understanding of God, revealed through all the variety of the present-day church. And it will certainly be necessary for us if we are going to develop the sensitivity and flexibility required to be able to express the eternal gospel in the many different cultures of the world.

The constant presence of study notes which reinforce a particular theological position can bring with it a reduction in our capacity to understand other points of view and truths in the Word which go further than these commentaries. We also run the risk of no longer reading and meditating on the biblical text itself, with the enrichment and greater intimacy with God that this presupposes, but simply reading it in conjunction with the interpretation offered by the editors of our Bibles. We make it difficult for the Lord to communicate with us or open our minds to new perspectives if we never allow him to speak to us without these printed interruptions, or if we silence the whisper of his voice with the shout and clamour of human opinions.

It is not that the interpretations we are offered in these notes are heretical or even inaccurate. They are normally the product of dedicated study by men and women anointed by God, and are sensible and balanced. They can be an extremely positive contribution to our understanding of the Word of God. However, their inclusion parallel to the inspired text limits our freedom to allow the author of the Bible himself to offer us his own commentary. We find ourselves imprisoned by one particular interpretation, and deaf to all that the Lord may want to say to us through these texts.

That's enough generalities; let's look at one specific example – Acts 1:8. This text expresses the central theme of the whole book of Acts, the pivot around which the history of the early church revolves. It deserves careful analysis. It is also known to be one of the fundamental texts for the modern Pentecostal movement, together with other key verses from the same book of Acts.

It speaks about the 'birth' of the church, and the stage entrance of the third person of the Trinity. Although he has been present with the disciples (John 14:17), as he had been with the saints of Israel (Judges 14:6; Psalm 51:11), now he takes on the role of protagonist. He fills their lives to overflowing. Acts 1:8 is linked with the 'gift my Father promised' mentioned by Jesus in verse 4, and with its literal fulfilment in the pouring out of the Holy Spirit in chapter 2. His effects are seen in the evangelistic activity of the apostles in the power of the Spirit throughout the whole book.

So far we are all in agreement, but a few crucial questions remain. What is the primary focus of this verse? What does it communicate to us? How should it be interpreted? What is the central emphasis which God wants to transmit to his church through this text? Is it the necessity of a second, personal experience after conversion, of baptism in the Holy Spirit? Is it the fact that power is received when the Holy Spirit comes into our lives? Is it the importance of witnessing, or the power of the Spirit to be witnesses? And where does 'Jerusalem, Judea, Samaria and to the ends of the earth' fit in?

What do the study notes of the Pentecostal Study Bible, published by Editorial Vida, tell us? Let us look at part of the extensive commentary offered to us (translated from the original Portuguese):

1.8 YOU WILL RECEIVE POWER. This is the key verse for the book of Acts. The main purpose of the baptism in the Holy Spirit is to receive power to witness for Christ in such a way that the lost will accept Him as Saviour and learn to obey everything He commands . . . The baptism in the Holy Spirit brings the personal power of the Holy Spirit into the life of the believer . . . The principal work of the Holy Spirit in witness and proclamation is to come upon believers so that they receive power and give testimony to the saving work and resurrection of Christ. . .

1.8 YOU WILL BE MY WITNESSES. The baptism in the Holy Spirit does not only impart power to preach Jesus Christ as Lord and Saviour, it also increases the effectiveness of this testimony through a relationship with the Father, Son and Holy Spirit which is strengthened and deepened by the filling of the Spirit . . . The baptism in the Holy Spirit gives power to testify about Christ and produces conviction of guilt because of sin, righteousness and judgement in the lost person . . . The baptism in the Holy Spirit can only be given to those whose heart has repented of evil works and turned to God . . . The baptism in the Holy Spirit is a baptism in a Spirit who is Holy. . .

A total of more than 600 words, but without any mention of the nations highlighted in this verse, nor of the 'ends of the earth'. It focuses on the believer's personal experience of the Holy Spirit, and the power which he brings to our lives, enabling us to give an effective witness to the person of Jesus Christ. The commentaries are absolutely right, but the absence of any allusion to the divine plan for world evangelisation leaves an enormous hole. Indeed, this concept does not get a mention until the note on Acts 2:4, commenting on the phrase 'filled with the Holy Spirit', with a sparse line in between hundreds of words dedicated once again primarily to the believer's personal experience of the Spirit. 'Pentecost is the beginning of world mission' is the only thing it tells us.

I repeat, there is nothing wrong with the commentaries quoted above. Within the framework of the doctrinal system of one sector of the church, they offer the believer a balanced application of what it means to be filled with the Spirit, and the important role of the Spirit in the work of testifying. But they leave to one side the idea of the expansion of the gospel throughout the known world; an idea which acts as the 'organising principle' of the book of Acts. And by offering themselves as a 'definitive' commentary on this verse, they have the effect of excluding this potential idea from the mind of the reader, and closing his or her vision to a harmony of the book of Acts, with its application seen in a commitment to missions today.

In Acts 1:8, Luke is not only talking about the vital need for an individual encounter with the person of the Holy Spirit for our well-being as believers and our effectiveness in personal witness. As well as that, he offers an 'outline' for the development of his account of the growth of the early church, a foretaste of the unfolding of the story of how the gospel was preached throughout the Roman Empire. It serves as an 'index' or 'contents page' for the rest of the book.

And to make it even more significant, we need to be quite clear that we are not talking about the whim of a human author. Acts 1:8 *is* inspired by God. We catch a glimpse here of the priorities in God's heart. He is revealing to us his desire for the message of salvation in Jesus not to be restricted to one people or one geographical area, but to reach all of humanity, to the furthest points on this earth, even touching the Samaritans, traditional enemies of its guardians at that time. Neither does it permit the disciples, a handful of Galileans, to bypass the capital of their nation, Jerusalem, or the surrounding area of Judea, despite feeling looked down upon and rejected by their inhabitants. Nathan's question to Philip on hearing about Jesus for the first time, 'Nazareth! Can anything good come from there?' (John 1:46), was applied by the Judeans equally to the whole region of Galilee.

This is why the field of operation of the disciples, once filled with the power of the Holy Spirit, begins in Jerusalem. In contradiction to what we hear and teach, Jerusalem was *not* the home of the disciples; that would have been Tiberias, Capernaum or Caesarea Philippi. With the exception of Judas Iscariot, Jesus' disciples were all from Galilee and the majority of Jesus' ministry took place in that region. After the resurrection he met with them there (Matthew 28:7, 10, 16; John 21:1). Those who witnessed his ascension into heaven were Galileans (Acts 1:11). Wisely Jesus had begun his ministry with people from one ethnic group, but at the same time prepared them for their future cross-cultural ministry. Jerusalem was not home for them; rather, it was the first strategic point in their campaign to conquer the world. To speak today of 'our Jerusalem' as

if it were the city in which we live is to ignore Jesus' clear
missionary intentions in sending his disciples there.

The book of Acts demonstrates careful selection in the
information that has been included, and only relates what
is essential, exclusively what contributes to the central purpose, which is to demonstrate the growth of the church and
its extension throughout the Roman Empire. It begins with
the Pentecost 'bomb' in Jerusalem. Who was affected by
this explosion of divine power? The priests and inhabitants
of the holy city? No! To start his church, God chose the festival of Pentecost, a date on which Jerusalem would be
packed wall to wall with pilgrims from all parts of the
Mediterranean world. He pours out his Spirit and the disciples begin to speak in other languages, as the Spirit enables
them. Let's read how Luke relates the effect of this event:
'Now there were staying in Jerusalem God-fearing Jews
from every nation under heaven . . . each one heard them
speaking in his own language . . . "Then how is it that each
of us hears them in his own native language?"' (Acts
2:5–8).

This would be enough, but no. Luke wants to 'go in for
the kill' and make sure that the reader has grasped what
God wants to communicate, so he continues: 'Parthians,
Medes and Elamites; residents of Mesopotamia, Judea and
Cappadocia, Pontus and Asia, Phrygia and Pamphylia,
Egypt and the parts of Libya near Cyrene; visitors from
Rome (both Jews and converts to Judaism); Cretans and
Arabs – we hear them declaring the wonders of God in our
own tongues!' (2:9–11).

It's quite a list. What detail! He gives specific mention of
each of these nations so we can see that the pouring out of

the Holy Spirit was for the benefit of the peoples of the world. The first impact of the gift of tongues was not for personal blessing, but to give testimony to the nations of the earth, a sign of God's immense desire for every creature to hear the gospel. The Holy Spirit comes to the people of God, and the peoples of the world are the first to receive his blessings. God is starting as he means to go on.

The narrative of Acts continues in the same vein. The first chapters tell of the expansion of the gospel in Jerusalem and the neighbouring villages (2:41, 47; 5:16; 6:1, 7), the first significant point in the expansion from Galilee to Rome. From chapter 8 onwards Jerusalem is not mentioned, apart from her influence on what is happening in other parts of the world – Peter and John go down from there to Samaria (chapter 8); Saul is presented to the apostles there (chapter 9); Peter returns there to give a report about his experience of preaching the gospel to the Gentiles (chapter 11); Peter is freed from prison there and John Mark is introduced (chapter 12); a meeting is called there to deal with those who are upsetting the work among the Gentiles (chapter 15), and finally Paul arrives in Jerusalem to be arrested and embark on his journey to the capital of the empire, Rome.

The book of Acts is not the history of the church; it is the history of the expansion of Christianity. It is not interested in the numerical growth of established churches, but rather in the opening of new fields of action. Once Jerusalem is taken, the focus changes. We don't need to know what is going on there any more, and it leaves the stage, along with its main protagonists. We are introduced to a man called Saul, and the believers begin to spread themselves throughout

Judea and Samaria, even if it is only because of persecution (Acts 8:1). A tremendous revival breaks out in Samaria, but not even a revival should stop the advance of the church: God takes Philip, the pillar of the work in Samaria, and sends him to a place in the desert to preach to an Ethiopian official. Having believed, the official carried on his journey and, according to tradition, became the founder of the church in his country. And Philip? Does he go back to Samaria to take up his work there? No way. He is taken away by God and, finding himself in Azotus, 'travelled about, preaching the gospel in all the towns until he reached Caesarea' (Acts 8:40), that is to say, along the whole Palestinian coast. Those who have the privilege of living in areas where there is revival should learn from the attitude of Philip and the priorities God demonstrates through his servant.

Samaria has been reached, and now it's the turn of the Gentiles. But how is a Jewish sect going to impact the heathen? Historian and doctor Luke tells us the story. He tells in great detail the conversion of a key figure for the work among the Gentiles, the Pharisee Saul (chapter 9), whose testimony is repeated twice before Roman governors. Even Peter is travelling in Judea, visiting brothers in Lydda, Sharon and Joppa (Acts 9:32–43), breaking down not just geographical barriers but socio-cultural ones too. (No practising Jew would enter the house of a tanner.) There, in Simon's house, God compels him to open his eyes to the Gentiles and almost two chapters are dedicated to the conversion of Cornelius and his family, the firstfruits of the non-Jews (chapters 10–11). Luke loses no time in telling us the next step, which takes place in Antioch, where some believers from Cyprus and Cyrene have arrived and 'proclaimed the message to Gentiles also, telling them the Good News about the Lord Jesus. The Lord's power was with them, and a great number of people believed and turned to the Lord' (Acts 11:20–21 GNB).

The 'neurological centre' of the church moves to Antioch, and the next push towards Rome comes from here, in the hands of the apostle Paul, at first under the tutelage of Barnabas. City after city, and then region after region, receives the gospel; the Gentile believers multiply, and some are included in the apostolic teams. Cyprus, Pamphylia, Pisidian Antioch, Iconium, Lystra, Derbe, Galatia, Mysia, Macedonia, Greece, Asia . . . the list of conquests grows, in spite of battles lost (Athens, for example) and casualties suffered (John Mark). Finally we reach Rome itself, passing through the courts of more than one civil governor. By the time the story is broken off, the Roman Empire has bowed the knee at the name of Jesus Christ, the only Saviour.

This is the story of which Acts 1:8 is the key verse, the story of God's blessing poured out for the nations of the earth. It is not a question of receiving an individual blessing from God, but of receiving his blessing so that we, in turn, can be a blessing to the nations. Another study Bible, the *Plentitud* ('Fullness') version, published by Editorial Caribe, comments on this verse as follows (translated from the original Spanish):

> *The commission and final promise of Christ, World Evangelisation.* In five references in the NT, Jesus directly charges his disciples to go and preach the gospel to all the world (Matthew 28:18–20; Mark 16:15–18; Luke 24:45–48; John 20:21–23; Acts 1:8).

Here the Great Commission is preceded by his promise to pour out the Holy Spirit. The endowing of power for evangelisation at world level is inseparably linked to this promise. Evidently it is necessary to receive this power if people are really going to come into the fullness of the gospel. But, before this, there is something else that needs to be resolved. The Holy Spirit has come to convince us that we need to go. We need power to be able to serve effectively, to heal the sick and release those who are possessed by unclean spirits. We need to receive the first anointing of the Holy Spirit, that is, to be able to act, to go. In this way the Lord will give us: (1) power to seek the lost; (2) authority to declare with energy that Jesus is the Son of God; and (3) power to establish his church locally and through the length and breadth of the world . . . The last commandment Jesus gave here on the earth has as its manifesto the power and the will of God to fulfil the task of world evangelisation (John 20:21–23; Acts 4:1–12).

The book of Acts ends, if one can speak of an end to this story, with Paul under house arrest in Rome, the capital of the most powerful empire ever seen on the earth. With this as a backdrop, Luke finishes with two awesome statements. First, he indicates the direction the future evangelistic movement will take and at the same time prophesies its success: from that point forth, 'God's salvation has been sent to the Gentiles, and they will listen!' (Acts 28:28). The message of Christ would be preached to the Gentiles, the nations, and they would accept the Messiah whom the Jews had rejected.

Secondly, it opens a door for the story to continue in the same way. We serve a God who opens doors no one can shut, and closes doors no one can open (Revelation 3:7).

There in Rome, in spite of being imprisoned, Paul 'boldly and without hindrance . . . preached the kingdom of God and taught about the Lord Jesus Christ' (Acts 28:31). Nothing and no one can hinder the work of God in the hands of his servants as they take the Word of salvation to the ends of the earth. The inexorable advance of the kingdom of God cannot be stopped.

And so we reach the end of Luke's narrative, but the story continues. He almost finishes in mid-sentence, indicating that the true story of the expansion of the church carries on up to today; the book of the Acts of the Apostles has 28 written chapters, but in his heart God has written chapters 29, and 30, and 31. . . And those who feature in these chapters are not the 'big names' of the church, the well-known preachers, but rather those who contribute directly to the extension of the gospel according to the scheme revealed in Acts 1:8, to the ends of the earth.

While there remain places where the Lord is not yet known, while the gospel still has not been preached in 'all nations', the end will not come. And the book of Acts will continue to be written. Peter, John, Philip, Barnabas, Lydia, Paul, Priscilla and Aquila, Apollos, Luke himself . . . they are all there, and many, many more. There are still chapters to write and names to add to the list. Will you be among them? What a joy it would be to read our names in that book, and know that we had contributed, in however tiny a way, to the expansion of the church among the nations of the world.

'Lord, here I am, send me. I will take your glory to the nations.'

17

'And Finally, Brethren'

'This is the end of the matter,' a wise preacher once said, 'you have heard it all' (Ecclesiastes 12:13, REB). And so it is. We have reached the end of our time together. Thank you for your company, and I hope it has been worth the effort coming thus far with me.

Allow me to finish with one final observation. We have dedicated many pages to those aspects of our Bibles which are 'not inspired', but always with the desire to discover the divine message which the Bible offers us. In the end our aim in all of this ought to be to uncover the full meaning of the Word of God and commit ourselves to obeying it. Nothing more and nothing less.

It is not our job to try to demolish any particular belief or conviction. Our mission is rather, with the same sincerity and honesty which we want to have on that day when we are before the throne of God, to seek to know his Word and put it into practice. Our disagreements over certain doctrines and practices, or our lack of understanding of certain other aspects, do not matter that much to God; what matters to him is our obedience to what we *do* understand of his Word.

While living for those brief years among us, allowing his own life to be an example of how we too are to live, Jesus made his intentions for his church very clear. Before he left, he transmitted a series of simple instructions to regulate our lives as believers, our relationships with members of the body and our relationships with those 'outside'. And since that time he has not communicated anything which would make us think he has changed his mind, or that these instructions are no longer valid. Nothing of what he later imparted through his Spirit to the New Testament writers in any way alters any of Jesus' instructions. On the contrary, these are confirmed through the apostolic testimony and through the example of the early Christian community, who took seriously their responsibility as worshippers and witnesses of Christ.

Among these guidelines for our behaviour we find the well-known 'Great Commission'. In fact, it was the last thing Jesus said to us before he ascended to his Father. You don't need a doctorate in theology to decipher it – a child could understand it perfectly. God has given a commission to his church, to be carriers of the message of salvation in his Son to the whole world, announcing it and teaching what it means to live as his followers, until everyone has had the opportunity to respond personally to God. It's that simple.

It's not our place to argue about whether this applies to us or just to the apostles, or to ask ourselves if we need a special call before we get involved in 'missions'. What he expects from us is that we, as faithful servants, obey the last orders we received as his church until further notice.

Almost 2,000 years later, there is still a world to be won.

There are still whole people groups who have not heard the name of Christ, and an increasing number of individuals who have not heard the gospel, and will not hear it if the church of Christ does not change its priorities. Since the day of Pentecost, God has had to struggle with a people who will not accept the agenda he has established and prefer to march to the beat of their own drum. Those who take his last orders seriously have always been a minority, and still are today.

But something is changing, and the church of Christ is growing faster than ever in the non-Western nations, which are waking up to their missionary responsibilities. After years of dependence on 'imported' missionaries, of evangelistic vision which did not stretch any further than the borders of their own country, they are hearing with an awakened ear the cry of the heart of God for his lost world. They are starting to take Jesus' last orders seriously.

'I call you friends,' Jesus says to us, 'because I have told you everything I have heard from my Father' (John 15:15 GNB). As I said before, it's not the parts of the Word of God we *don't* understand that matter; it's what we do with the parts that we *do* understand. Our obedience to his orders matters. 'You are my friends if you do what I command' (John 15:14 GNB).

The kingdom of God will not be spread throughout the earth by words, theories, missiological models, or whole libraries full of books like this one. It will be in obedience to Jesus' simple command, by men and women of God anointed with the power of the Holy Spirit and zealous to see his glory among the nations. But it starts with obedience to the will of God revealed in the last command Jesus gave on earth. Our compassion will not motivate us – we have hard hearts and do not respond to the evident need around us. Neither will the cries for help we hear stimulate us to preach the gospel. It must be in simple obedience, the giving of our lives to the task that most moves the heart of God – seeking out the members of the bride for his Son from among all the nations of the earth.

With this challenge we reach the end – the challenge of obedience to the clear and simple message of the Bible regarding world evangelisation. It is in our hands. 'Now that you know these things, you will be blessed if you do them' (John 13:17).

Postscript

Imagine that by this stage my unrepentant missionary bias will have become more than evident. I make no apologies for this – it has been central to my understanding of the Christian faith ever since I came to Christ while working as an interpreter in Paris, where I soon saw that there was a greater purpose to my life than making money.

It is my prayer that this work may serve to fan into flames in its readers a similar passion for seeing God's glory across the nations of the world. If the first sparks have begun to catch in the kindling of your own heart, then I would be delighted to help you explore the means of seeing where that may lead.

For myself, starting with a short-term trip into North Africa, then growing through ongoing informal involvement while training and working as a teacher to full-time, long-term service in Spain, World Horizons has been the ministry where my missionary commitment has found expression over the last two decades and more. Here I have found the freedom to explore the potential of my own calling within the security of a prayerful and visionary community, equally determined to see Jesus Christ named in the remotest parts of the earth.

Today World Horizons is an international movement of some 300 people spread through 30 nations of the world. Our aim remains the same – to transmit to God's people, wherever they are, his heart for the nations of the world, to equip those who want to be part of the answer for effective cross-cultural work, and to pursue relevant and culturally sensitive pioneer ministries under the leading of the Holy Spirit as he directs. Details of our UK-based programmes can be found at www.worldhorizons.co.uk. And if I can be of any help to you in understanding and pursuing your own calling, do not hesitate to contact me on NeilRees@worldhorizons.co.uk

Appendix

Resources for Understanding the Bible Better

Most of this book has been given to looking at some of the dangers associated with the different 'helps' that are included in our Bibles. However, it is not my aim to discourage anyone from drawing on these helps to increase their understanding of God's Word – far from it. I would rather seek to encourage their right use, in order that we may better hear from God, and do his will.

Although ultimately we are right to interpret Scripture by Scripture, a series of basic tools is necessary to enable us to read the Bible in the same way as its original recipients would have understood it. *Sola Scriptura* is fine, as long as we are talking about the source of authority for our faith. But none of us will properly understand our Scriptures without going outside them for some background and guidance. Written for people so far removed from us in time and space, we simply cannot expect to understand its message to them fully without this.

Some like to find as many of these helps as possible within one volume – the famous 'study Bibles'. While these are undoubtedly useful, particularly to have access to a smattering of information at least in our Bibles, there is a limit to what can be included in one printed volume. Such a Bible can never include a complete concordance, for example. Serious study really does demand that we invest in separate works. The following pages give some guidance in choosing elements to make up this 'basic tool kit' for Bible study.

First of all, though, we need to decide what translation of the Bible to use. Personally, I recommend the Good News Bible or New Living Translation for general day-to-day reading, and the New International Version for study. Whatever you choose, do not rely on just one translation – get used to comparing various readings to make sure you do not miss anything. If you want to understand a bit more about the whole process of Bible translation, the difference between dynamic equivalence and literal translations, and so be able to take a more informed decision about which Bible to use, I would recommend the following as a complete and readable guide:

• Duthie, Alan S., *How to Choose Your Bible Wisely* (Carlisle/ Swindon: Paternoster Press/Bible Society, 1995)

Once we have chosen a few translations to work from, the very minimum we need is a **Bible handbook**. **A Bible dictionary** is also a good starting point. Invest in a few books, or some computer software. You will find a number of good resources – though don't rely on what is on a CD without knowing something about the authors. Choose recent editions where possible, and always ones that are backed up by good evangelical scholarship (some are produced by very liberal scholars who seek to demolish evangelical convictions, and others by evangelicals with little regard for good scholarship!), such as:

- *The Holman Bible Handbook* (Nashville: Holman Bible Publishers, 1992)
- *The Lion Handbook to the Bible* (Tring: Lion Publishing, 1973)
- *The New Bible Dictionary* (Leicester: IVP, 1962)

Other basic tools include a **Bible atlas**, and some kind of **theological dictionary**, such as:

- *The Harper Concise Atlas of the Bible* (New York: Harper Collins, 1991)
- Richardson, Alan (ed.), *A Theological Word Book of the Bible* (New York: Collier Books, Macmillan, 1950)

A **concordance** is useful for thematic study, though not needed for exegetical study of whole books – I would suggest using *Strong's* or *Young's*, as both have reference to the original languages and enable further study. (The disadvantage is that both are based on the King James Version – use *The NIV Complete Concordance* if you are more familiar with that version, and leave the others for further reference only.) For those wishing to trace word studies through the original languages, computer programs linked to Strong's numbering system are perhaps the easiest to use, and enable searching for a phrase as well as individual words. For printed concordances of the Greek and Hebrew linked to Strong's numbers use:

- *The Word Study Concordance* (Illinois: Tyndale House Publishers, 1972)

- *The New Englishman's Hebrew Concordance* (Massachusetts: Hendrickson, 1984)

Concordances are OK for word study, though for study of a theme you need to make sure you find all related terms too. **Thematical indexes** are useful for this, one of the best available at present being:

- *The NIV Thematic Study Bible* (London: Hodder & Stoughton, 1996)

To understand some of the 'problem passages' of the New Testament, and much of the prophetic material of the Old, in the end we will need to consult a **commentary**. (This should only be done, however, *after* an initial attempt to analyse a book – we should become familiar with the biblical material before seeing what others think.) A one-volume commentary will not give the kind of detail that is needed for serious study, and will often in fact only do what we should do ourselves as readers! We really need to look at an individual commentary on each book if we want to get the most out of a passage, though building up a collection of commentaries on individual books can be expensive. A good one-volume commentary can be a useful initial reference tool, particularly if you have access to other volumes when needed. As one of the better one-volume evangelical commentaries I would suggest:

- Elwall, Walter A. (ed.), *Evangelical Commentary on the Bible* (Grand Rapids: Baker Book House, 1989)

For individual commentaries, Fee and Stuart's book (see below) contains a list of recommended commentaries for each book, or try ones from the following series:

- *Tyndale Old/New Testament Commentary Series* (Leicester: IVP)
- *The Expositor's Bible Commentary* (Grand Rapids: Zondervan, 1982)

Once we have access to these basic tools, we will be well equipped for Bible study. Now let's look at a few other resources which can help us by giving us needed background information.

Understanding the Bible starts with knowing how to read and study Scripture for ourselves. The following guide to inductive study is quite a comprehensive manual for this:

- Morey, Earl Wesley, *Search the Scriptures* (Virginia: Agape Ministry, 1993)

The following books give principles for understanding and interpreting Scripture, and I would particularly recommend Fee and Stuart's excellent book:

- Fee, Gordon D. and Douglas Stuart, *How to Read the Bible for All Its Worth* (Grand Rapids: Zondervan, 1981)
- Briggs, Richard, *Be an Expert in 137 Minutes in Interpreting the Bible* (Bletchley: Scripture Union, 1998)
- Berkeley Mickelson, A., *Interpreting the Bible* (Grand Rapids: Eerdmans, 1972)
- Sproul, R.C., *Knowing Scripture* (Downers Grove: IVP, 1977)

Computer software can be a great help, though some programs, while very good, are also very expensive. The website 'e-sword' provides completely free downloadable software, and contains some excellent resources beyond the biblical text itself, such as the full version of the *International Students' Bible Encyclopaedia* and *Vine's Dictionary of New Testament Words* – almost all you will ever need as reference material. I would highly recommend this program. The Online Bible is inexpensive and of good quality, and the Unbound Bible is a good web reference resource.

- Free downloadable Bible software (www.e-sword.net)
- The Online Bible for Windows (www.onlinebible.org)
- The Unbound Bible (www.unboundbible.org)

For an introduction to the subject of the canon of Scripture, and the process by which the Bible reaches us, from inspiration, through original manuscripts, to translation, see:

- Geisler, Norman L. and William E. Nix, *From God to Us* (Chicago: Moody Press, 1974)

For those interested in the subject of textual criticism, and understanding the variant readings of the New Testament, use the following in conjunction with the United Bible Society's fourth edition of the Greek New Testament:

- Metzger, Bruce M., *A Textual Commentary on the Greek New Testament* (Stuttgart: United Bible Societies, 1971)

It is extremely helpful to understand something of the background of the Bible too. For the Old Testament, Walter C. Kaiser Jr is an evangelical scholar whose writings bring very helpful insights. The following make a good starting point:

- Kaiser Jr, Walter C., *Toward Rediscovering the Old Testament* (Grand Rapids: Zondervan, 1987)

- Kaiser Jr, Walter C., *Toward an Old Testament Theology* (Grand Rapids: Zondervan, 1978)

There is abundant literature on the New Testament, and we certainly do need to understand the background to life in first-century Palestine to make sense of Jesus and his teaching. Everett's material is particularly comprehensive, while Malina's work provides valuable insights into the social structure of the New Testament world:

- Ferguson, Everett, *Backgrounds of Early Christianity* (Grand Rapids: Eerdmans, 1987)
- Lohse, Edward, *The New Testament Environment* (Nashville: Abingdon, 1976)
- Jeremias, Joaquim, *Jerusalem in the Time of Jesus* (Philadelphia: Fortress, 1969)
- Malina, Bruce J., *The New Testament World: Insights from Cultural Anthropology* (Louisville: Westminster/John Knox Press, 1993)
- Malina, Bruce J. and Richard L. Rohrbaugh, *Social-Science Commentary on the Synoptic Gospels* (Minneapolis: Fortress Press, 1992)

For an excellent introduction to each New Testament book (looking at content, author, date and place of writing, audience, composition, textual difficulties, and ideas from recent scholarship), Carson, Moo and Morris's book is hard to beat; the two dictionaries are excellent reference works that deal deeply and thoroughly with matters that arise in the Gospels and Paul's writings:

- Carson, D.A., Douglas J. Moo and Leon Morris, *An Introduction to the New Testament* (Grand Rapids: Zondervan, 1992)

- Green, Joel B. and Scot McKnight (eds), *Dictionary of Jesus and the Gospels* (Leicester: IVP, 1992)
- Green, Joel B. and Scot McKnight (eds), *Dictionary of Paul and His Letters* (Leicester: IVP, 1993)

For studying the synoptic Gospels, some kind of synoptic presentation is very helpful, and many are available. These are normally arranged in vertical columns, but I find the following horizontal analysis much easier to use and thus more helpful:

- Swanson, Reuben J., *The Horizontal Line Synopsis of the Gospels* (Pasadena: William Carey Library, 1975)

The following are of particular help in understanding how Jesus thought and spoke, Ladd's book giving an excellent overview of Jesus' concept of the kingdom of God:

- Stein, Robert H., *The Method and Message of Jesus' Teaching* (Philadelphia: Westminster, 1978)
- Ladd, George E., *The Presence of the Future* (Grand Rapids: Eerdmans, 1974)

For background on Paul and the situations in each of the cities and churches to which he wrote, see:

- Bruce, F.F., *Paul: Apostle of the Heart Set Free* (Grand Rapids: Eerdmans, 1977)

For a one-volume commentary on the book of Revelation, I have found this one particularly helpful:

- Wilcock, Michael, *The Message of Revelation*, The Bible Speaks Today Series (Leicester: IVP, 1975)

Bibliography

Deere, Jack, *Surprised by the Power of the Spirit* (Grand Rapids: Zondervan, 1996).

Editorial Vida, *Biblia de Estudo Pentecostal* (São Paulo: Vida, 1995).

Harper/Caribe, *Biblia de Estudio Harper/Caribe* (Nashville: Caribe-Betania, 1997).

Rattray Hay, Alexander, *The New Testament Order for Church and Missionary* (Argentina: The New Testament Missionary Union, 1964).

Index of Scripture References

Old Testament

208 NOT EVERYTHING IN OUR BIBLES

Judges
14:6 .182

Ruth
book of Ruth 120

1 Samuel
book of 1 Samuel 119
3:13 .146
7 23
24:3 .127

2 Samuel
book of 2 Samuel 119
6:22 .146
19:43 146

1 Kings
book of 1 Kings 119
7:23 .127
12:4,9–10 146
14:24 158

2 Kings
book of 2 Kings 119, 120
19:35 141
21:9 .159

1 & 2 Chronicles
books of 1 and 2 Chronicles . . . . .
    119, 120

Ezra
book of Ezra 119, 120
2 142

Nehemiah
book of Nehemiah 119, 120
13:25 166

Esther
book of Esther 120

Job
book of Job 120
1:8 165
8:4 164
11:6 .164
15:5–6 165
16:21 35
34:7–8,35–37 165

Psalms
1:1 127
2:8 129
8:2 128
8:5 129
9:8 160
10:1 .168
13:1 .169
18:49 160
21:1,13 128
22:27–28 160
23 167
25 20
28:7–8 128
34 20
37 20
40 67
40:6 .129
47:1 .160

Subject Index

NIV Life Application Study Bible

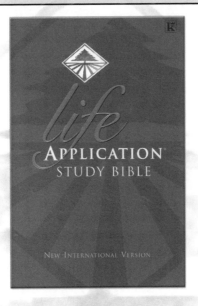

The world's most practical study Bible, with over 10,000 application notes, charts, timelines, personality profiles, and a topical lining index - all designed to help apply the Bible to life.

NIV Life Application Study Bible HB
ISBN: 0854769463
Price: £24.99

Also Available in Bonded Leather:

Black: 0854769498
Burgundy: 085476948X

Other Hardback *versions:*

Indexed: 084234893X
Large Print: 0842348956
Large Print Indexed: 0842348964

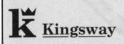
Kingsway